D1242177

THE
BOOMERANG
EFFECT

HOW YOU CAN TAKE
CHARGE OF YOUR LIFE

NICOLA BIRD, PhD

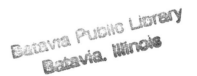
IUNIVERSE, INC.
BLOOMINGTON

The Boomerang Effect
How You Can Take Charge of Your Life

The information, ideas, and suggestions in this book are not intended as a substitute for professional advice. Before following any suggestions contained in this book, you should consult your personal physician or mental health professional. Neither the author nor the publisher shall be liable or responsible for any loss or damage allegedly arising as a consequence of your use or application of any information or suggestions in this book.

iUniverse books may be ordered through booksellers or by contacting:

iUniverse
1663 Liberty Drive
Bloomington, IN 47403
www.iuniverse.com
1-800-Authors (1-800-288-4677)

Because of the dynamic nature of the Internet, any Web addresses or links contained in this book may have changed since publication and may no longer be valid. The views expressed in this work are solely those of the author and do not necessarily reflect the views of the publisher, and the publisher hereby disclaims any responsibility for them.

Any people depicted in stock imagery provided by Thinkstock are models, and such images are being used for illustrative purposes only.

Certain stock imagery © Thinkstock.

ISBN: 978-1-4502-8722-7 (sc)
ISBN: 978-1-4502-8724-1 (dj)
ISBN: 978-1-4502-8723-4 (ebk)

Printed in the United States of America

iUniverse rev. date: 2/9/2011

Dedicated to my beloved Jasim, and the special people who have
journeyed alongside me

CONTENTS

Introduction

This book is designed to help you take more charge of your life. You will be given the tools to help better manage the challenges you face on a day-to-day basis, so you can live a happier, empowered, and struggle-free life. If you have ever wrestled with negative thoughts, confused feelings, and relationship issues, or notice that the same problems resurface, you know what it is to feel stuck. I created this book to show you how you can change unhealthy patterns and feel more in control of your life, starting with yourself. The result: more harmony and wellbeing, and overall life improvement.

The ideas presented here are primarily based on my almost two decades of work as a psychotherapist, practicing the method that I pioneered and introduced to the world in the early 1990s called Self-Imaging Therapy™, or SIT. SIT is a transformative inner process—very much like an active, therapeutic meditation—that helps people overcome their problems and live the best lives possible. SIT achieves maximum results quickly and deeply, because it changes people from the inside out and gives them the tools to heal. In the many years that I have been practicing my SIT technique, I've watched countless people transform their lives, starting from their very first session with me. I've seen depressed clients learn to feel optimistic; anxious people learn to be calm and nonreactive. The anecdotal reports from my clients attest to the benefits of the therapy, as they report a greater sense of personal control, power, peace, and self-confidence. They learn to be more kind and loving to themselves.

We all encounter problems. Who of us does not experience difficult circumstances, situations that upset our day, challenging relationships, negative thoughts, messy emotions, and painful memories? Every person will find that they repeat negative patterns or that the same problems continually resurface. Most of us desire to gain greater control over our lives and free ourselves from the blocks that hold us back and stifle our potential. Learning how to successfully manage the many conflicts we encounter, which is what this book is about, helps us to feel more in charge of our lives, even as we face all kinds of disruptions, be they minor or major.

The circles of repetitive stress, strain, and strife that we experience are what I refer to as *the boomerang effect*. This is when we find ourselves struggling with similar problems that we long to liberate ourselves from. These can be inner conflicts, such as feelings of inadequacy, shame, imperfections, hurt, or anxiety. Or they can be external challenges, such as relationship troubles, professional issues, weight battles, or financial woes.

The Boomerang Effect explains why and how you get trapped in negative cycles. It then provides you with the tools to overcome these obstacles and take charge of your life, starting with yourself. These ideas and techniques are derived from my SIT principles and methodology. I've written this book in a user-friendly style to help you can gain deeper self-awareness and insight. By seeing and understanding what goes on at typically unconscious levels, you can break free of the mental boxes that inhibit your life.

This book is the result of the journeys of my clients and the knowledge that I have amassed from them throughout the almost twenty years of my SIT practice. It is also a reflection of my own inner processing, insight, and development. As the creator of SIT, I am the original guinea pig—change always starts with me. I am sharing the tools that I designed to help my clients and me empower and enrich our lives, so that you can improve yours as well. You are en route to discover how you can take charge of your life and liberate yourself from stress, strain, and struggle. The end result: more peace, joy, and personal power.

boomerang:

—noun
1. a curved flat wooden missile of native Australians, which can be made to return to thrower
2. an action or statement that recoils to its originator

—verb
3. to come back or return, as a boomerang
4. to cause harm to its originator; backfire[i]

1: The Boomerang Effect

The game of life is the game of boomerangs. Our thoughts, deeds and words return to us sooner or later, with astounding accuracy.[ii]

A boomerang is a curved wooden missile that goes back to its thrower after being hurled, returning to its point of origin. Its rotation is circular: round and round and round it goes. Do you ever feel that way about your life and experiences? That you are caught in a loop of sameness? You find that you're encountering similar situations, relationships, thoughts, and feelings, which wouldn't be bad if these were happy things. But when they're not, when they create stress, struggle, and strife, we can feel like we're stuck in a static universe that regurgitates the same problems back to us. This is what I call *the boomerang effect*: the circle of problems—challenging emotions, thoughts, conflicts, and dramas—that turns back up in our lives.

The stress that we encounter doesn't usually make for sunbeams, rainbows, or cotton candy. It's more like hiccups, or gum stuck to the bottom of our shoe, or the neighbor's blasting music, or tomato sauce on our new white shirt, or biting insects—all the mucky, murky, and messy stuff we experience. And that's why I call the unfortunate matter of stress and strife the *muck factor*. The word *muck* is traditionally defined as "dung, quagmire, bog, chaos, confusion and trash".[iii] Chaotic, confused, bogged down, and crappy—mucky—are certainly things we feel when faced with life's more tedious and irksome ways.

The muck factor, then, is the sum total of all the problems we encounter. It's the negative thoughts that run amuck in our mind, the "I'm not good enough" or "I can't do anything right" mental tapes. The chaotic emotions we grapple with—such as inadequacy, shame, worry, loneliness, confusion, anger, hurt, or fear—are part of this muck-factor family. It can feel mucky to us when we face challenging situations, like financial pressures, testy relationships, or stressors at work. Personal issues—isolation, weight gain, poor self-image, failure—all fall under its umbrella. Painful memories are other things that muck us up. These are the experiences that have hurt us, such as abandonment, betrayal, rejection, criticism, and loss. The muck factor can rob us of deeper meaning, personal power, connection, and purpose. We find ourselves looking and longing for spiritual fulfillment, understanding, and satisfaction, grasping for answers but only finding more questions. Our essence feels incomplete, calling out for more substance and wholeness. We suffer a loss of self and feel like we have no power in our lives.

Essentially, what we perceive to be the negative issues in our lives are those things that feel like the muck factor to us. We end up frowning when we want to be smiling; procrastinating when we need to be motivated; afraid when we long to be brave; negative, not positive. Instead of calm, we're anxious, angry, or powerless. Rather than seeing the joy and light, we observe the misery and darkness. Our soul longs to sing and dance, to be free.

You will undoubtedly be familiar with the muck factor—I know I am—whether it is in your life a little bit, somewhat, or a whole lot. It's always around, lurking either close by or in the distance. An unavoidable and often unpredictable part of existence, that's what the muck factor is. There's always some random problem that we have to deal with every day of our lives: the kids misbehaving, bad traffic, a miserable boss, too many dishes, lonely nights, not thin enough, no time.... Yes, indeed, the muck factor can be a most disagreeable thing to bear. Weighty and burdensome even at the best of times, at its worst, the muck factor can make us feel like we're trapped in a universe of never ending darkness. When it feels as if there's an overwhelming amount of it in our lives, life loses its spark and joy. Our spirit is compromised. We're disconnected from ourselves. There is no sense of control.

So no, we're not fond of the muck factor and its boomerang effect. Random and capricious, it creeps into our lives, usually without us even realizing that it's coming to get us. It's always around in some form or another. Then, before you know it, it stresses us out, even robs us of happiness, if only for a moment or two. The unfortunate thing about the muck factor is that there's so much of it around. Everywhere we look, there it is: someplace where people are starving, in our community where people are losing jobs or fighting injustices, in the unhappy faces we see on the streets, among friends in bad relationships or in miserable jobs. Most of all, we see it in the measure of our lives, the ways we think and feel about ourselves, our purpose, and our relationships. Pervasive and ever present is the very nature of the muck factor, and there are all kinds of ways that we can experience it.

THE LAYERS OF STRESS, STRUGGLE, AND STRIFE

Essentially, the muck factor is anything that creates strife or struggle for us, and no, it doesn't matter if this strain is a little or a lot. It will still have some negative impact on us and get in the way of our feeling good, perhaps to the point where it can be difficult to move forward with our lives. Our potential is compromised. The muck factor is particularly lethal due to its random, inconsistent ways and its constant presence. We never quite know when and where it will pop up, but we certainly understand that it will appear again. Additionally, it can come and go in waves, turning up out of the blue, when we are least prepared. So we can be feeling pretty good and managing well; then something shakes up our world, like relationship issues, an officious new office manager, or clothes that are suddenly tight. In a matter of seconds, we go from okay to not so okay. The muck factor's chaotic, capricious, but ever-present nature adds another layer of strife for us, because predicting or controlling it is impossible.

Whether it is as minor as feeling unsettled and dissatisfied, or as severe as being unable to find a happy or calm place inside of us, we all need to look at the omnipresent muck factor throughout our journey of life. Certainly, we will always encounter it, as it never goes away. And unfortunately, we can't get away from the reality that the muck factor creates problems. This means that we are forever faced with the daunting task of figuring out how to manage or cope with the many challenges that life continually throws our way. We need to know how to deal with those challenges, so we can feel more in charge of our lives. That is what this book is all about.

MARY'S BOOMERANG

"I want to get rid of my problem," says Mary, a frustrated young woman in her late twenties. "Why does it keep coming back? Why won't it go away? I think I overcome my issue, but then it appears again. I feel stuck and powerless. I just want it to disappear."

Mary is echoing a sentiment that I hear from people who seek my professional help as a psychotherapist: the desire to get rid of, or to hide from, or to conquer the conflict that is challenging them. The issue can be an external situation, like relationship or work difficulties, or an inner struggle, like anxiety, fear, or insecurity. Usually, it is a combination of both.

Mary's particular problem is relationship based. She finds herself stuck in romantic relationships that never go right. The men abandon her, she tells me. She feels deserted and alone. As she explains her dilemma, her focus is on the external circumstances that are causing her conflict. Most of her energy is spent ruminating about the terrible situations and people that life is handing her. She feels powerless in the face of her problem, especially since it recurs. She perceives difficult situations as things that happen to her; that they are not so much about her, but about what life is doing to her. When she does self-examine, she criticizes and blames herself for causing the problem; there is a sense of deep shame. For the most part, Mary doesn't know why the bad things keep happening to her, what is causing them, or what she did to deserve them. The underlying causes of the conflicts are often vague, even unknown. In those moments when she does achieve clarity, when she is able to connect the dots between her feelings of abandonment and her father's neglect, her reactions don't change all that much. Her habitual thoughts and emotions are still running her, and the situation manifests once more in one form or another.

Mary finds herself either overreacting to challenging situations, or reacting in ways that are less than beneficial. On the one hand, she is angry and resentful. On the other hand, she is resigned and complacent, making excuses and justifying behavior (hers and others). She believes she is trapped in her reactions to the problem, and thereby trapped by her anger, passivity, and sense of victimization. More often than she likes, she feels that her emotions and thoughts are controlling her, rather than she them. She is also caught up in other people's negative reactions to her; and she finds that she replays in her mind what they said and did that made her feel so bad about herself. Mary's reactions to her conflict are all over the place, and she is unable to bring them into order for any significant length of time. She feels scattered and unfocused.

The feelings and responses that Mary is experiencing as a result of her conflict are far from unique. I hear different versions of her same struggles from most of the people who come to see me. Many of us don't know the underlying causes of our conflicts or the deep-rooted issues that are affecting our perceptions and reactions. Even if we have some sense of the core reasons for our behaviors, thoughts, and emotions, we still find ourselves struggling with our reactivity. Like Mary, we don't see how it is possible for us to actually choose our emotional reactions, transform our repetitive mental tapes, and liberate ourselves from the recurring conflicts we encounter.

*

I help Mary and other people resolve their issues and empower themselves through a psychotherapy approach and process that I pioneered in the early 1990s called Self-Imaging Therapy™, or SIT. SIT is a deeply transformational and image-based method that has liberated countless people from their personal struggles. An inner, solution-driven process, SIT is a journey inside the self—very much like an active, therapeutic meditation—that targets and resolves the root of problems, for speedy results. People's negative self-images, such as the insecure parts of the self that impede personal growth, are confronted and transformed into positive ones that build self-esteem, inner peace, and strength. How does the image-based SIT create healing, change, and empowerment? Part of the answer lies in the mind's perception. The mind cannot distinguish the difference between what is real and what is imagined. If you vividly imagine biting into a sweet, juicy fruit or favorite dessert, you will salivate in the same way that you would if you were actually eating it.[iv]

So when people confront and transform their self-images through their imaginations, they experience the change as real and immediate. Time is inconsequential. They have the power to go back and rescue themselves from past hurts. They discover and strengthen positive things inside themselves that might have been hard to hold onto, such as confidence, calm, and self-worth. And their minds don't recognize that the imagination is not the "real" world. The minds' focus is only on the space and time that they are occupying; the moment is all there is. In this way, the SIT method enables people to develop deep, enriching relationships with themselves through self-care, transformation, and expanded perspective. They learn that they have the power to change, and that they can take charge of their lives.

FIGHTING, HIDING, AND RUNNING

Mary's story represents many of the ways we feel and react when faced with the challenges the muck factor poses in our lives, especially issues—whether they be emotional, mental, relational, or situational—that repeat themselves, thus exacerbating our stress and strife. Through her SIT sessions, Mary learned that the three ways she invariably tried to manage the conflicts she faced was by *avoiding them, hiding from them*, or *fighting with them*. She discovered that her habitual use of these coping styles created more problems than they fixed; but these responses were so much a part of Mary's patterns, inner dialogue, and mindset, it was hard for her to see them, much less change them. Indeed, what Mary's described as her three patterns of responses to perceived challenges—*avoiding, hiding,* and *fighting*—are generic and mostly unconscious reactions and mindsets that all people presented when going through the SIT process with me, often to their surprise, frustration, and chagrin.

In seeking resolution to her problems, Mary's strongest tendency was to run away and avoid the whole mess altogether. Her reasoning was that if she could escape the bad situation by replacing it with something happier, then the problem would disappear. For example, leaving a bad relationship for a seemingly better one, only to discover the new one is just an updated version of the old. She was simply recycling her predicament. But she also found herself fighting with the problem to make it better. In her efforts to resolve the issue, she struggled to control, conquer, and change it, usually by trying to fix the other person or situation, rather than herself. For instance, struggling too much with her partner to make him "get it," simply to find that there was strife and no resolution. Then there were times when she retreated from the troubling situation in her endeavor to pacify it. She hid behind a veneer of tolerance, masking her hurt, hoping that the conflict would have resolved itself by the time she came back out to face it. Hence, she would withdraw from her partner so that he could figure things out for himself, only to discover nothing had changed.

The unconscious and habitual ways we react to challenges is part of what keeps us trapped in the very thing that we are trying to free ourselves from, and robs us of our power. I have learned from my experiential SIT work with clients that the three reactions that Mary described—running, fighting, and hiding—are overused by nearly all of us; and they invariably keep us trapped in the boomerang effect. In other words, stuck in whatever problem(s) we face. We end up spinning our wheels looking for answers, but are left with more unresolved questions. Instead of being in control, we feel more out of control.

Because we are mostly unaware of these habitual thought processes, we can have difficulty liberating ourselves from the circle of stress and struggle we encounter. We end up feeling stuck or trapped in the boomerang effect. In this book, you will learn about these particular mindsets, so that you can be more aware of what you're typically unconscious of, and thus feel more empowered to direct your life. I use anecdotes and vignettes to demonstrate these ideas. They are primarily taken from my clients' SIT sessions. Through these, you will understand how the ways you think, feel, and react to your challenges can perpetuate problems. This awareness will enable you to create change in your life, and provide you with a greater sense of personal choice and power. I will also give you tools to help you manage these ingrained responses to further empower yourself. In this way, you will learn how to navigate through the stress, strain, and strife you encounter with less conflict and greater liberation, leaving more room for the positives of life, like clarity, calm, harmony, fulfillment, and joy. You will have the ability to take greater charge of your life, starting with yourself.

RECAP OF KEY CONCEPTS

the boomerang effect: Finding yourself trapped in the vicious circle of well-worn stresses, emotions, problems, struggles, and dramas that just haven't changed.

muck: The challenges in life that weigh us down, things like messy emotions (e.g., insecurity and fear), negative thoughts (e.g., "I'm not good enough"), difficult circumstances (e.g., financial stresses, challenging relationships), and painful memories (e.g., past hurts and betrayals).

muck factor: The muck factor is what makes us feel like we're bogged down in the dirty, dank trenches of life.

THE FIGHTER

2: Mi-mi the Fighter

If you want peace, stop fighting. If you want peace of mind, stop fighting with your thoughts.[v]

Imagine this scenario: You feel rejected. Your lover's neglecting you. This hurts. It's not the first time this has happened, not the first time you've felt like this in your relationship. Rage boils inside you because the problem is occurring *again*. You're cursing at your partner in your mind, fuming at the abandonment. You can't stand it when you get treated like this. You're angry, confused, and frustrated. Your partner is making you feel bad, your irate mind fumes. He is ruining your day. The reaction that is bubbling up inside you—indeed taking over—is the drive to fight and conquer this problem. Your claws are out, sharp and ready to raze this situation to the ground. You've had enough. You need your lover to get it, to get that this is not the way to treat you. And you know how to resolve this particular obstacle. You're going to *fight* this battle of the neglectful partner, so you can overcome this conundrum and regain control once more. Then you'll feel good again. Yes, conquering this issue is the answer to your problem.

In the above vignette, like Mary (in chapter 1), you want to fight the muck factor in an attempt to conquer and control what you *perceive* as its onerous presence. Indeed, there's a fighter, in varying degrees and forms, in all of us. Since an essential aspect of reducing the boomerang effect is self-awareness—to become more conscious of the ways we manage the problems in our lives—and since struggling and battling with our challenges in an attempt to overcome them is something we all do at times, we will explore the fighter reaction.

So let's take a look at how you might deal with the abandoning partner, whom you feel is mucking you up, when you are in the battling mentality of a fighter. We'll call your neglectful and wayward partner *Mucky,* to represent the muck factor that is being triggered by his behavior. You will be *Mi-mi the Fighter,* to represent your reaction to the muck factor. The vignette or short story below depicts one manifestation of a fighter's mentality and reaction to conflict.

MI-MI THE FIGHTER IN ACTION

Your mind is racing. Your day started out well enough. Like a clear glade or open, sunny field, you were feeling pretty good. Then Mucky abandoned you. Again! He *shouldn't* be like this. Now everything's changed and you're irritated. No, downright angry. Mucky is the one that did this to you, that's what you're thinking. Just when you believed he'd changed some of his wayward ways, here he is again and everything's gone sour. Now it feels like your day's turned cold and bitter. And it's all *Mucky's* fault. *He* makes you feel this bad. *He* is to blame for you being wretched all of a sudden. *He* shouldn't behave in this way.

"*That's it!*" you think. "I've had quite enough of Mucky doing this to me. Mucky's bad ways destroy my happiness. He should behave better than this." You tell yourself you're going to make him get it this time. That's the answer to your problem. You imagine your victory. Set to slay this particular dragon, you say your bit to him in your strongest and most assertive voice, taking no nonsense. But … he's just not getting it. In fact, *he's* angry at *you* for being so unreasonable. He doesn't see your point or agree with what you're saying. You're the problem, not him.

"This is unreal," your mind is screaming. "What the $%&*#@ …?" Your head is getting crammed with war scenes as you become increasingly frustrated and angry. How can he not get it? Why is he like this? The Fighter in you is more stoked than ever. The situation is driving you crazy, and you can't let go.

"Don't let him get away with this," the Fighter voice in your head insists. Your mind is running amuck while Mucky (the devil in your mind now) is sitting in front of the TV, remote control in hand, seeming as pleased as a pig in the muck. The more powerless you feel, the angrier you get, and the more dismissive he appears to be. You can see he's not going to "get it," but you can't seem to let go or stop yourself. The Fighter in you is taking over, overriding all reason and rationality. You hate the powerlessness you're feeling because he is still neglecting you. You need to protect yourself from that.

So you're back to trying to overcome Mucky's ignorance and neglect, fighting to be acknowledged. You want to feel better, and if he'd just get it, then you would. But struggle and battle though you may, there's no getting through to him. You feel progressively worse now, a loser. Not only do you feel abandoned by him, but you feel bad about yourself. You're not good enough. Your mind is on overdrive, screaming in rage, although no coherent voice is emerging. The battle is now located in your head. You're angry at him, but you're also blaming yourself for being so stupid. You're tired, but the struggle within is worsening. The war inside of you is in full swing. You can't let it go....

THE FIGHTER'S TRAP

Why did you get stuck in this continual battle? Why did you keep fighting even when you realized it would lead to no victory? A part of the reason has to do with the primitive brain. The impulse to fight what we view as threatening—the muck factor, in this case—is written into our DNA. The primitive or *reptilian brain*, which is part of the limbic system, reacts to perceived danger by fighting the source of the threat, so that it can be subdued or conquered. It is a rapid-fire, automatic response that occurs in nanoseconds. We are programmed, so to speak, to struggle. It is part of our genetic makeup, preverbal and unconscious, designed to protect us from the dangers of life. Many of the conflicts that threaten us are due to situational or emotional causes and mental perceptions:

1. The *situational causes* are the tangible things that we experience in the outside world, like criticisms and put downs from others; arguments with loved ones; or rejection, betrayal, or abandonment from an intimate person in our lives.

2. The *emotional causes* are the intangible things that we experience. These occur at the inner level of feelings. We feel such things as insecurity, shame, loss, hurt, embarrassment, fear, worthlessness, sadness, etc.
3. The *mental perceptions* or beliefs that lead us to interpret a situation, person, or feeling as threatening. We think that we are not good enough or strong enough, that we are not safe, that something or someone is bad or inappropriate, etc.

We struggle with both the people and things *around* us (situational causes) or the feelings and thoughts *within* us (emotional causes and mental perceptions) that mess us up. These feelings, perceptions, and situations will cause this primitive part of our brain to fight or struggle with the perceived threat, whether or not we are conscious of what we are apprehending as threatening. Fighting is our attempt to control or subdue the emotions, thoughts, problems, or person, so that they or he or she can be conquered. It's our way of problem solving. The reasoning that drives this is the idea that triumphing over the muck factor will mean we no longer have to deal with it. This will make us feel better, the reward at the end of our struggle. If you are *repeatedly* or *indiscriminately* reacting to the ever-present muck factor or one element of the muck factor—like your lover's neglect or a fear of abandonment—in the mentality of Mi-mi the Fighter, it means you possibly are doing one or more of these five things:

1. Struggling over and over again with the same or similar problems and getting nowhere
2. Struggling too much or indiscriminately with people and things around you
3. Too regularly or indiscriminately beating up on, criticizing, and blaming yourself, your mind in overload, or targeting others in your environment
4. Reasoning in terms of what *should be*, as in "It should be happier, better, more egalitarian …"

5. Seeing the world, others, or the situation as the cause of your pain and suffering.

THE FIGHTER'S WORLDVIEW

The Mi-mi the Fighter persona represents our inner dialogue and manners of functioning when responding in this primitive mode. This is the mentality of the fighting instinct within us. I give this part of you a personality so that you can more easily see yourself. Self-awareness is one of the first things we need in order to overcome the boomerang effect. If we have a strong, well-oiled fighter habit, it will feel as if it just takes over. Positive rationalizing, relaxing, letting go, and other such beneficial attitudes will be harder to implement when we are focused on protecting ourselves. Neither will we notice that we're getting beaten. The need for control or to conquer overpowers us. We get lost in this manner of "reasoning."

When you are dealing with the muck factor from the Fighter perspective, you will notice that you are struggling too much. This struggle may occur within you by being too hard on yourself, or by arguing in your mind with the image of the person or thing you perceive as causing your stress. Struggling can also extend into the world around you, where you find yourself battling too much with others and circumstances—arguing with your partner, raging at your circumstances, and the like. The fighting mode makes you think in terms of what "should be," as in, "She shouldn't behave that way," "I shouldn't feel this way," and "The world shouldn't be so messed up." And then we want to right the wrong of how we think it "should be."

You need too much control over situations, your emotions, or others when you are in the Fighter mode. You are overly invested in winning and conquering, to the detriment of letting go. Emotions like anger, annoyance, and frustration are prevalent. There is a lack of flexibility and fluidity. You resist change; you're closed to other possibilities. Your way or the highway is the thinking. Letting go and surrendering will be difficult. You need to control the things, people, and situations in your life, or make things better. You dislike feeling vulnerable and open, as it means giving up control, something to which you are most attached.

You hate losing. In the extreme, you are rigid, closed off with anger and rage at yourself, the world, and others for perceived injuries.

Mi-mi the Fighter:
Characteristics: controlling, conquering, overdoing, resistant, biased, stubborn
Reasoning: "It should be."
Mantra: "It must be conquered."
The Result: struggling, rigidity, limited, stuck, stunted, angry, self-blaming, frustrated
Antidote: surrender, softening, letting go, giving in, being "wrong," humility.

Recap of the Key Concepts

emotional causes: These are feelings that cause us to respond in the primitive mindset of fighting. They occur when emotions like insecurity, shame, loss, hurt, embarrassment, fear, etc. are triggered within us.

mental perceptions: These are the beliefs that lead us to interpret a situation, person, or feeling as threatening. We think, for example, that we are not good enough or strong enough, that we are not safe, that something or someone is bad or inappropriate, etc.

Mi-mi the Fighter: The personification of the fighting part of you. This aspect of you copes with what you perceive as challenging by trying to control, conquer, and subdue.

situational causes: These are the situations that cause the primitive response of fighting. Examples are criticisms and put downs from others, an argument with a loved one, or rejection, betrayal, or abandonment by a romantic partner.

3: The Story of Mercy the Fighter

Mercy the Fighter[viii] is an artist in her early forties. When she first came to work with me, she had been battling a debilitating depression. Having gotten a better handle on it from doing the SIT process with me, she is now ready to tackle the low self-esteem that contributes to her depression.

"I am very critical of myself," she tells me. "I always see the wrong in what I do, never the good. It makes me feel bad about myself. I now realize this leads to my depression, because it makes me feel low and down, uninspired and hopeless. I want to get rid of this part of me."

"Let's look at this inner critic," I say.

"I feel the critic inside my head," she explains as she closes her eyes. She is beginning her SIT process. She is breathing deeply, and with her mind's eye she is looking inside herself. "It feels like it is the core of my brain. I visualize it as bullets shooting everywhere in my head. It's a battlefield in there—like a war zone—and I can't get out."

"What happened to make your brain like this?" I ask.

"It's all I know. My brain's been like a war zone since I can remember. It comes from my father's criticism: hearing that I couldn't do anything right and feeling that I wasn't good enough because of it. The bullets represent the critical names he called me and the put downs—all the negative energy. I haven't gotten them out of my head. They're stuck there, and it's now the way I treat myself. It is like my father's critical voice has become my own. I feel powerless and helpless against it. I try to fight it, but I can't beat the self-critic. It's greater than me. It's all I know; it's a part of me now. I can't stop the war zone image that I have inside my head. It's more powerful than me. That's what it feels like."

"Let's not think in terms of fighting the inner critic as much as retraining this part of you to grasp a greater reality of self-love, self-understanding, and self-compassion. Low self-esteem is what you learned, not who you are. There's more to you than this. You can learn to see yourself in a positive light by teaching the critical part of you how to be loving, kind, and supportive."

"As odd as this might sound," she responds, "I feel a resistance to this idea. My chest tightens and feels like a hard block. Although I want to take control of the critic and the negative thoughts—what I visualize as bullets—there is resistance. I know this sounds crazy, but part of me wants to stay there and protect it. It feels like home. It feels uncomfortable to be anywhere else but here. It's all I know. There's a high to the self-beating, like drinking or drugs. It is how I drive and motivate myself. I don't think I'll be able to accomplish anything or be a responsible adult if I do not beat myself into shape."

"That's because you never learned a gentler, kinder, more loving way to manage your challenges. You don't understand that self-worth is the greatest motivator of all, because this has not been a part of your reality. But you can learn this now."

"I do see that there is no merit to the self-beating. Not only does it *not* motivate me, it actually does the opposite. It paralyzes me. It leads to my depression. So it's not working. I need to change, but I am afraid to. Some part of me believes that the self-criticism works, although yes, I now know it is an illusion. But what if the other way is worse? I'm afraid to try something else. In my mind, this self-beating gets results. It drives me along and helps me accomplish things. I won't act if I'm not angry with myself. I'll just be lazy and do nothing."

"The association is false," I say, "but again, it seems that way because you have never been fueled or driven by your sense of self-worth in any significant or long-lasting way."

"I don't know how to really love myself. I don't know what that is. I don't know that I can change."

"Once you are open, then this is possible," I say. "You need to stop protecting your inner critic and be open to loving yourself."

I take Mercy the Fighter through the process of breathing into the low self-esteem that she holds inside her body, a technique that teaches her how to relax through her discomforting emotions. (See chapter 13, exercise 1 and exercise 4, for similar techniques that you can do on your own.) "Now let's connect you to your sense of worth," I say. And I take her on that journey.

*

It is hard at first for Mercy to claim her worth when her sense of inadequacy is so strong. This is further exacerbated by the "high" she gets from self-beating, which she considers motivational. She wants to protect her inner critic, as we can see by her resistance to changing it. This is how she remains trapped in the boomerang effect. That is a key part of the self-awareness that comes from doing SIT. Mercy the Fighter would have vehemently denied there was any reward from her self-beating. She would maintain that she just wants to get rid of it. Going deeper inside herself, she learns she is stuck because of her attachment to the very thing she is trying to change. She is protecting this harmful part of herself. In this way, she stays cocooned in her known world of self-criticism.

I go on to show Mercy how to find worth within herself. (See chapter 13, exercise 2, for similar techniques that you can do on your own.) She feels this in her heart and imagines it as an ocean of water. As she opens her senses to experience and learn self-value, she is able to feel it emotionally and physically. This makes it more real to her.

*

Mercy the Fighter needs to actively work at feeding her self-worth and starving her inadequacy. There are many more resistances and distortions that we work at breaking through in follow-up sessions, but each week she reports a progressive feeling of self-esteem and a reduction of the inner critic. She is happier overall, sleeping better, and feeling more peaceful inside.

"I'm discovering different, more positive parts of myself," she tells me. "I appreciate myself more. Inside my head is more peaceful without the war being played out in there. I now know that I can find within me all that I need to be whole and complete."

THE HIDER

4: Mi-mi the Hider

The power of hiding ourselves from one another is
mercifully given, for men are wild beasts, and would
devour one another but for this protection.[ix]

Perhaps you're thinking that you're not so much of a fighter when it comes to dealing with your perceived problems. Sure, you get that way sometimes, but that's not how you typically deal with your stress and strife. If your lover rejected or hurt you, for instance, fighting is not what you'd normally do. That would be your last course of action. You don't think it does much good to keep fighting and battling, for the problem will keep perpetuating itself. When it comes to managing your problems, you relate more to the response to *hide,* which Mary talked about in chapter 1. This is the impetus to retreat from conflict, rather than struggle with it, so that it doesn't affect you. Why fight when you can hide so that problems can't find you? That way you can live a peaceful, happy existence. Makes sense, right? That's the answer to your problems. Let's call this part of you *Mi-mi the Hider.* In your mind, hiding is a much better way to manage challenges, because it gives you an out from your stress. Let's say, once again, that your lover—whom we'll also call Mucky—is neglecting you and that's a problem for you. Here is one enactment of the way you would respond to this unsavory situation, when in the mindset and mode of Mi-mi the Hider.

Mi-mi the Hider in Action

Imagine this scenario: Your morning began happily enough when, out of nowhere, Mucky is not there for you when you need him. Your deep disappointment shakes you up. Worse, he's making you feel bad about yourself, not good enough. You distance yourself from him and withdraw. You retreat to a place in your mind where you can cordon yourself off from these hurtful sensations. It feels like a dark, closed off place inside of you, where you feel happier—in your mind, that is—because you've separated yourself from the pain. Yes, you feel a bit numb even as your mind is racing, analyzing the situation, but that's better than being overcome with disappointment at Mucky's terrible behavior. You don't have to feel too much when you shut down. It's safer, the answer to your problem, right?

While in retreat, your mind's abuzz, thinking, "What if this keeps happening?" You need to make sure abandoning Mucky doesn't continually bring you down and make you feel bad about yourself. So the Hider in you has the perfect solution. Don't get too excited or happy about the relationship. Mask and hide those feelings, because he's going to keep doing this. Since you don't know when this could happen again, you need to be ready, on high alert, just in case....

But the next day, when Mucky turns on his charm and is attentive, he drags you out of your retreat, pulling you back out into the open. You're passionate and excited. But shortly thereafter, when he's neglectful and you feel abandoned once more, you plummet.

"Okay, this openness will *never* do," you tell yourself. "I have to protect myself more. I'm not hidden enough. I never know when Mucky will reject me again and make me feel unimportant." You withdraw even more from the bad situation, though your mind is fixated on what more could happen, ready for the worst. This is your Hider's way of not having to feel hurt from Mucky's neglect. Anticipating the worst will protect you from the pain of his potential wrongdoing, is what you're thinking. It keeps you watchful and alert. That way, Mucky can't take away your joy when he rejects you again. The Hider in you worries constantly about *what if* Mucky neglects you again. Projecting these negative expectations into your future, you imagine all the terrible things that could happen.

Hiding, however, has a price. It is a dark state, a static world where nothing can grow. Withdrawn, alone, and isolated, you feel the very pain you want to hide from. But the Hider in you doesn't see it that way. Although it's scary and lonely, hiding still seems safer than getting hurt by Mucky's abandonment again. Yes, you are more resigned to the negativity, and your anxious mind is constantly preparing for the worst. Still, you reason—in the most paradoxical kind of way—that this ruminating keeps the negativity out. You see, the Hider in you feels much worse being exposed and out in the open, where Mucky's abandonment can damage you. Yes, you might feel like you're losing yourself, your truth, and authenticity, hidden as you are behind this mask of tolerance, but the Hider in you sees that as preferable to the pain of abandonment. The world of Mi-mi the Hider is dark, but it is safe.

THE HIDER'S TRAP

The second primitive or "reptilian" response to perceived threat is the freezing[x] impulse. Animals freeze or camouflage when they want to protect themselves from danger. In the same way, it is part of our DNA to deal with conflict and threat in this manner. We try to manage the inner emotional causes (e.g., hurt, rejection, abandonment, neglect, insecurity), the mental perceptions (e.g., I am not good enough; they are mean), and the outer situational causes (e.g., criticisms from or arguments with others) by hiding from these perceived threats. Mi-mi the Hider is the persona that represents our inner dialogue and reactions, when we try to manage the muck factor from the hiding perspective. Mi-mi the Hider symbolizes this mentality. Thus, if you are *repeatedly* or *indiscriminately* reacting to the muck factor in the manner of Mi-mi the Hider, it means that you are doing five possible things:

1. Regularly masking your hurt and pretending that everything is okay
2. Frequently or indiscriminately retreating from the challenging situation, so that you can get away from the pain for as long as you can

3. Often numbing yourself by shutting down your uncomfortable or vulnerable feelings, so you don't have to feel bad about yourself
4. Reasoning in terms of *what if*, as in, "What if the world ends?"
5. Seeing the world, others, or the situation as the cause of your pain and suffering; you are powerless.

THE HIDER'S WORLDVIEW

Hiding is a numbing state, born as it is of freezing. We are withdrawn, distant, and removed; camouflaged and masked. Being invisible is a comfort zone when hiding. It means we will not be seen. The outer world and its inhabitants cannot get to us or hurt us, so we feel safe and protected. We won't have to experience shame, criticism, rejection, etc. At least that is the illusion of the impulse. The hiding part of us sees it as a way not to feel our own painful emotions. We believe it enables us to not only hide from the precarious world around us, but also to retreat from having to deal with our own messy emotions and issues. That means we are hiding from ourselves.

When you are in Hider mode, you will feel numb and shut down, blank and not present. You will not be open. You will have the urge to cut yourself off from the world and others, so you push away a potential relationship or give up trying to get the new job you want. Hiding gives you the illusion of safety. You have a greater sense of control in a universe that seems unpredictable and random.

Masking your emotions, thoughts, and self so that others won't hurt you gives you that illusion of control. You are apt to wear a persona, like that of a pleaser or rescuer, so others cannot really see you or know you, and thus damage you. You might also use this persona to gain approval for the pretend self. That way you can hide from your self-loathing by getting validation from others. As a result, hiding will eventually make you feel like you are losing yourself and can't be who you truly are. The mask you're wearing to hide your feelings, thoughts, and self will have become too thick and concealing.

When hiding to cope with the muck factor, you will be more easily resigned and down on life, expecting the worst. It will make it harder to move forward and take risks. As a result, you will wallow in the very thing you are trying to hide from. You won't trust yourself or others, believing it is better to hide than be hurt by the outside world. Your reasoning will be in terms of *what if*, as in "What if the aliens invade?" or "What if it doesn't work?" When you are strongly in the hiding mode, you can get easily pulled into states of depression, victimization, powerlessness, anxiety, and most of all, isolation.

Mi-mi the Hider:
Characteristics: safe, withdrawn, victimized, hidden, distant, closed off
Reasoning: "What if …?"
Mantra: "It is what it is."
The Result: masking, loss of self, helplessness, powerlessness, victimization, resignation
Antidote: openness, connecting, revealing, vulnerability, truth.

Recap of the Key Concepts

Mi-mi the Hider: This is the hiding personification that helps you cope with what you perceive as challenging by masking, retreating, and numbing.

5: The Story of Mark the Hider

Mark the Hider[xi] is seated before me. Things aren't going too well, he tells me. Job's gone, girlfriend's MIA, and he has no idea where he's going and what to do with his life. Lost. That's the word he uses to describe himself. He feels displaced and despairing. Hopelessness is grabbing onto his brain cells and squeezing them like an old, wet sponge. It's hard to see any of these problems just by looking at Mark. He's educated, well-dressed, and articulate. Nothing on the outside indicates his current state of confusion and chaos. He wears his mask well.

"I don't get it," he laments. "How did my life disintegrate like this? Why am I here? I feel like I try so hard."

"Let's see what's happening inside of you," I say. "What do you feel?" And so he turns his attention inward to places deep within, where the mind's eye doesn't usually reach. This is his SIT session with me.

"I feel sadness. It sits in my gut. There's a concentration of sadness at the base of my belly that weighs me down. I visualize the sorrow as heavy and solid, like stone. I'm sad from many things that happened to me throughout my life: loss, hurt, rejection. This sadness is familiar. It goes way back to the beginning of my life. I've always known it."

"Your sadness feels like stone to you?"

"Yes, my sadness weighs me down. At least that's what it feels like. But at the same time, the stone that I visualize forms a shield around my body, keeping everything distant from me. Nothing and no one can get through it, so it keeps me isolated. The aloneness feeds my sadness and perpetuates the problem. I am protecting myself from sadness, and that protection keeps me sad."

"This is a circle of sadness." *The boomerang effect,* I think. "Sounds more like you're insulating the sadness rather than shielding yourself from it."

"That's true. The shield isn't working. It's keeping me sad. It is creating what it's supposed to prevent."

"What is the shield supposed to be protecting you from?"

"The outside world, the unknown, because I don't know what I could encounter and experience. I'm afraid to be abandoned. The shield hides me from everything."

"So you are stuck in your known world of sadness, trying to protect yourself from an unknown world of expected sadness?" I ask. "You are afraid of sadness, but since it already exists inside of you, you can't protect yourself from it. It is now a part of you. And to compound the problem, you're afraid of the world's potential to make you sad. That's one big circle."

"Part of life is sadness; it's a natural component of existence," Mark says. "But sadness is now a part of who I am. Because of what I've experienced, I strongly identify with it. With time, it's gotten more concentrated, because I haven't ever fully let it go. If my world contained all emotion, little particles of everything—things like happiness, peace, and disappointment—I would be filled up with these different emotions. There wouldn't be so much sadness inside of me weighing me down. But sadness has taken over. It consumes too much space inside of me. The rest of me feels empty. In trying to compartmentalize the sadness from the rest of me, it just made it all worse."

"Why are you compartmentalizing?"

"I want to separate from the sadness inside of me and not have to feel it. I don't like feeling it. It brings me down, and I want to get rid of it. So I'm compartmentalizing to control the sadness, but it doesn't work. It is inside of me and has nowhere to go. I'm stuck in it. The more I sequester it, the more it grows and takes over. I understand that the inside of me needs to be filled with the spectrum of everything. That is the healthier way of being. But who wants to feel sadness? That's the problem. I keep wanting to hide from this hurt and get away from it. When I hatched this system, I thought I could control this bad feeling by putting it in a corner, but it doesn't work."

"You need to be able to feel and work through everything and not avoid your hurts," I say.

"I feel like there is no way out anymore. The weight of this sadness—what I visualize as rock—is impenetrable. It is so much a part of who I am. I can't get out."

"This is not who you are, just what you learned to be. There's so much more to who you are that you have not realized, because the sadness took over. But as you pointed out, there is a lot of space inside of you for everything to exist. You can connect with this and feel more complete, rather than identifying so much with this one small part of you that is sad."

"I have lost so much of myself. How do I find me again?" he asks.

"Imagine breaking through the rock that you visualize as your sadness. Imagine that you can take control of it and dismantle it and let it go. You are controlling and directing it, rather than it controlling you."

Mark the Hider breaks down his barriers. (You can do a similar process for yourself by following the techniques outlined in exercises 1 and 4 in chapter 13.)

"That really works. Everything is lighter," he states.

"Now visualize a time when you felt confident and secure. Reenact that time. Where do you feel that?"

(See exercise 2 in chapter 13 for a similar technique.)

"In my heart. It feels like a bright light, warm and vibrant. It makes me feel strong and safe—and happy."

"You need to get to know this confident part of you more, to nurture it to bring out its potential and strengthen its presence in your life. This confidence is also who you are, and it hasn't been lost. It is within you, a part of you. You need to claim it and give it more attention. Starve the sadness, feed the joy."

*

The images create change for Mark the Hider, because the mind/body doesn't know the difference between what is real and what is imagined. He is able to apprehend a different worldview, from one of powerlessness to one of self-direction. Mark works hard at developing and strengthening this newfound security inside himself. The sadness is strong and returns, but with time and effort, he is able to refocus and build contentment from within. Life changes for him as he feeds his sense of safety. He no longer feels as lost and confused, and has more power to shift those feelings. He's found missing parts inside himself that make him feel better about who he is. When he stopped holding the world responsible for his sadness, he stopped making the world responsible for his happiness, and nurtured the positive within. He took back his power. He began a new career and is working to repair his broken relationship.

THE RUNNER

6: Mi-mi the Runner

All human beings should try to learn before they die
what they are running from, and to, and why.[xii]

Perhaps you find that, like Mary, although you relate to or react to the stress of the muck factor by fighting or hiding, there's something else that you typically do to cope. Your way of reacting is to escape from the problem and find a better place to be. If you felt abandoned by your lover, you'd rather get away from the problem—not have to deal with it—and be somewhere happier, rather than struggle with or hide from it. You have more control when in running mode; you get to a place that is brighter. Now that's the answer to your problem. This is the mentality of the Runner in you. We'll call that part of you *Mi-mi the Runner*.

Let's say that your abandoning lover is once again called Mucky. And when he gets out of hand, you get far away from the bad situation and your hurt feelings as fast as you can, so you can be in a better, happier place. Indeed, there is another fellow who's looking pretty good. His name is Glade, and he is light, bright, and clear. You'll escape Mucky and replace him with the attentive Glade. That will ensure that the problem goes away for good. No more negative emotions to deal with. Gone will be the terrible pain of abandonment that Mucky causes. Let's explore how the Runner in you manages the challenge of an abandoning partner.

Mi-mi the Runner in Action

Picture this scenario: Your day was off to a good start. You met this great guy named Mucky, and he set your world on fire. He's The One, for sure. He makes you feel good. But then you start noticing that Mucky is not as wonderful as he first appeared to be. He has this way of neglecting you and making you feel not good enough and insignificant. You are hurt and abandoned. You play out scenarios in your mind of the day when things will be better. *If only* ...You're still feeling crappy, though. You need to get away from all this rejection misery. So off you run to your happy spot by the beach, where you can feel good about yourself again. There you get attention from some of the guys hanging around, and that makes you feel like you're special. They affirm your value. That's the answer to your problem.

Mucky, you soon realize, is all over the place: attentive today, neglectful tomorrow. So you're spending quite a bit of time escaping to your happy place, where you don't have to deal with the wretchedness that Mucky's abandonment causes. Then one day, out of nowhere it seems, you meet Glade, who is the antithesis of Mucky. He's attentive and makes you feel as good as Mucky once did. Hey, you can get away from Mucky and go to Glade. The perfect solution to the conflict, the real answer to your problem. My, oh my, how bedazzling Glade is! Trumpets and harps play, and you joyously race around with Glade. Nothing is as sweet as Glade; nothing makes you feel as good about yourself as Glade. You've always longed for someone like this glorious Glade to come along and rescue you from all the bad in life. Your mind is filled with romantic scenarios that make you feel wanted and loved.

Not too long after escaping the abandoning Mucky to consort with the attentive Glade, you notice that Glade's changing. He has a shadow around him that's making him look kind of like Mucky. But that can't be. Instantly, your mind denies these thoughts and focuses on how great Glade is, running from this negative picture. Images of Mucky's abandonment pop into your mind, but you ignore them. Instead you reenact the day you met Glade and how wonderful he was then. Glade's full of potential.

But things really are changing. Glade's not around like he used to be. Actually, he's beginning to look a lot like Mucky. Funny how you didn't see that before. Then you discover that his real name is Mucky, and Glade's the moniker he used to seduce you. So now you need to get away from this *same* problem of abandonment. Again! *If only* Mucky would change and just behave his bad self, your mind screams. So you're back to running off to a brighter place, looking for something to rescue you from the bad feelings you're experiencing again about yourself—that you're not good enough—as a result of the recent abandonment.

"*If only* I could find the real Glade," you dream. So you escape the latest Mucky and go looking for a new Glade to rescue you from your feelings of inadequacy and aloneness. And that's when you meet *him*. Feeling good about yourself again because of the attention you're getting from him, you finally ask his name. "Mucky," he tells you. Funny how you always meet men with that name. But this Mucky is different from the other two. So you're running down the road with him, not noticing that he is disappearing before you even reach the corner.

THE RUNNER'S TRAP

Mi-mi the Runner is the personification that represents the third primitive brain response written into our DNA: the flight response. Getting away from the things that can harm us ensures our survival. Mi-mi the Runner personifies this escapist mentality. It is the instinct to run away from what we perceive as threatening, so that we can arrive at a better "reality." We don't want to deal with the things that negatively affect us. We try to get away from the emotions, thoughts, situations, and people that disrupt us; try to escape to a place that we believe is better. Thus, if you are *repeatedly* or *indiscriminately* reacting to the muck factor or an element of the muck-factor in the manner of Mi-mi the Runner, it means that you are doing five possible things:

1. Perpetually escaping to something you deem as pleasurable so that it can rescue you from your problems and make you feel happier, like alcohol, drugs, food, shopping, partying, relationships, work, etc.
2. Too often denying how badly you feel or how terrible the situation is, and sugar-coating it, believing it is okay

3. Regularly avoiding the entire problem as much as you can, so you won't have to get upset, feel bad, or deal with it
4. Reasoning in terms of *If only*, as in "If only things would change," in the hopes of being rescued from the challenges you face
5. Seeing the world, others, or the situation as the cause of your pain and suffering.

THE RUNNER'S WORLDVIEW

When we are functioning from the perspective of Mi-mi the Runner, we will respond in escapist ways to what we perceive as threatening, be that emotional (perhaps dealing with feelings of hurt), mental (e.g., the belief that we don't measure up), or situational (lover abandonment or withdrawal). If we can always get away, we are safe. It gives us the feeling of being in control and powerful in a world that is decidedly unpredictable and erratic. The muck factor, capricious though it is, can't reach us, because we've gotten away from it. We create realities that don't exist to help us escape the world, thoughts, or emotions that we find problematic. To help us escape, we make up *if only* realities so we can avoid challenging emotions, perceptions, and situations. For example, we dream of being rescued from loneliness by the perfect lover. Or we imagine the day when we will be thin or rich. Thus, you can substitute food, mind-altering substances (alcohol, marijuana, etc.), clothes, gambling, work, and so on, for the character Glade in the vignette above. That is, if your lover abandons you, and you feel inadequate as a result, you use food, alcohol, shopping, or the like to make you feel good. Whatever you run to will be something you perceive as rewarding, and will provide you with a sensation of associated happiness, even if only for the moment. The Band-Aid for a gaping wound.

When you are in the running mode, you will have the tendency to create stories out of air that you then project into the future. It's never about today; always about tomorrow. If you are afraid of something, you will project negatives and try to protect yourself from them. Thus, if desertion is your fear, you will imagine your new partner is abandoning you. You will see this in his or her smallest, most innocent actions, and will feel the need to protect yourself from it, destroying what is good in the process. Conversely, if you are longing for something to fill the holes in your soul—say, love—you will only see what you want to see. For instance, you'll highlight the positives and ignore the negatives in your lover to support your idea of what you need. The Runner in you is either anxiously trying to protect you from potential pain—thus projecting doom—or trying to help you escape your pain by projecting an indiscriminating positive. Running mentality obscures your ability to see the truth. You won't know what is real or imagined. Confusion abounds as you vie for control in a world and mind/body that is indeed messy and precarious. This is one of its most dangerous traits.

The running mode makes you addicted to the feel-good state. You won't like feeling what you perceive as negative, and thus you can never transcend it. You want to feel good instead of bad, so you'll keep trying to escape whatever you view as problematic. It will be hard for you to sit still and work through conflicts. Denial and fantasy take the place of reality. Living in the now is difficult. You'd rather be away from, instead of connected to, yourself. Life ends up being anywhere but the here and now.

Mi-mi the Runner:
Characteristics: escapist, avoidant, dreamer, ungrounded, dissociated, out there
Reasoning" "If only ..."
Mantra: "It could be."
The Result: all over the place, avoidant, addictive, never present, anywhere but here, denial
Antidote: stillness, quiet, grounding, being in the moment, reality.

Recap of the Key Concepts

Mi-mi the Runner: This is the running part of you that copes with what you perceive as challenging by trying to escape, deny, or avoid.

7: The Story of Mary
the Runner

"I'm stuck in relationships that never go right. The men don't stay with me. They leave. I feel abandoned."

Mary the Runner[xiv] is the warm, affable young woman in her late twenties whom we first met in chapter 1. She is at once attractive and inviting. Part of the fashion buying team for a retail outlet, Mary has a lilting, singsong voice that fills the room with a cheerful resonance, despite the sadness that lurks in its corners.

"What is it about me?" she cries. "What am I doing wrong?"

This is where her journey begins with me. She takes a deep, abdominal breath, along the lines of chapter 13, exercise 1, and closes her eyes to look within herself. She is in a SIT session with me.

"I'm a shadow of a person. This is how I visualize myself."

"What happened to make you like this?" I ask.

"Life has dictated it. All my past events have made me this way."

"Tell me what happened to you."

"I started becoming a shadow of myself when I was a child, when my father would disappear. He didn't love me. That's what the child in me thought. He said he did, but then he'd leave. I guess that's why I want all the control now. I want to rule. Without control, I have nothing."

"Tell me about this control," I say.

"I visualize myself being on a planet all alone. I'm running from the people who can hurt me. I'm isolated out of necessity, running away to gain power and control."

"Your conflict and pain is that you are lonely and abandoned, but you are calling control isolation. You are feeding the very thing that you are trying to change."

"It makes no sense. I'm running away so no one can hurt me by abandoning me, but the running means that I am alone, so it hurts me. What I am is stuck. The irony is that the running makes me feel strong. In my mind, I'm running things, but really I'm just running *from* things. I thought I was running away from the problem to a perfect world, but the truth is that this alternate world is actually another version of the same problem. The original plan was to run to something else, but what happened was the hamster wheel. So I got stuck there. I lost sight of what I was running to. I want control, but in reality I have no power. The problem remains the same: I feel abandoned and alone. Nothing's changed."

"Why do you stay there?" I ask.

"I want to conquer this aloneness, but I'm afraid to go back to the real world. I don't know how else to be. This way is safe. I don't want to close the door on this safety. As strange as this may sound, I feel like I have some degree of control in my isolated world. I don't have it when I'm not there."

*

And so the boomerang goes round and round. Mary's protectionism makes her want too much control. She is trying to compensate for her lack of real power by striving for control. This traps her in the very thing that she is trying to run away from.

"Power is not about controlling everything or everyone around you," I say. "It is something within you that you cannot find by focusing on events, people, or things. It is discovering what is missing in your life and filling those holes in your soul. It is feeding your life from the inside out, taking care of self."

"How do I heal?" Mary asks.

"Where is the pain of abandonment inside of you?"

"In my heart. The image I see is a heart mired in muck. It's burdened with all the things that happened to me. It feels heavy, sad, and alone. It's not happy in there."

"What does it need?"

"Me to take the time to take care of my heart, to take care of me and not expect others to do that. I've always wanted to be rescued, but now I realize that I need to rescue myself."

"You can nurture your heart in your imagination. (See chapter 13, exercise 3 for similar techniques that you can do on your own.) It will feel real because the mind doesn't measure reality only in physical or external ways. The mind functions in terms of perception and perspective. Your heart will not care who loves it. It only wants to know love. You can give yourself that love. Through your imagination, you can connect with it. Imagine that you are hugging and massaging it, nurturing it and taking care of it as you would a baby."

"Wow, that works. I feel a sense of love and connection inside of me replacing the loneliness. I see that I can take care of me. My heart has changed. It is bright now. I feel more whole, and both feet are finally on the ground. I'm no longer a shadow. I feel what power is, and it is not control."

"What do you visualize power to look like?" I ask.

"It is golden, bright, warm sunlight. This is my new heart. I feel open and alive, connected to something powerful, strong, and positive within me. I feel complete, and I am okay."

*

Mary the Runner continues to work on her own, as well as with me, to feed her power and starve her fear of abandonment. A few weeks later, she walks more confidently into my office.

"I'm dating," she tells me. "I feel more self-assured, more open to life and living. I'm more aware of my controlling and needy behaviors. Instead of trying to make him fix me, like I used to do with men, I'm looking within more. I'm also not focusing on the negative as much. If it doesn't work out, I have more confidence that I can take care of myself. I feel freer to be who I am. I don't need to try so hard to prove myself. I'm happier inside, happier with me. I love me a whole lot more."

While Mary has not fixed all her problems, and dating anew will most certainly bring its own challenges, she has both more self-awareness and the tools to assist her in managing the difficulties she will undoubtedly face.

8: The Three Protectors

With chronic stress, you become more primitive.[xv]

Mi-mi the Fighter, Mi-mi the Hider, and Mi-mi the Runner are the personifications and mentalities that represent our three *protectionist responses*: fighting, hiding, and running—better known as the fight, freeze, and flight[xvi] reactions to perceived danger. Did you see any of yourself, your attitudes, reactions, behaviors, and perceptions, in them? I bet you saw a whole lot of you in these characterizations. That's because fighting, hiding, and running are our three primal responses when we are threatened by what we *perceive*—real or imagined, conscious or unconscious—to be the muck factor. We fight to control or conquer the problem. We run away so we don't have to deal with the issue. We hide, thereby masking the problem or preventing it from getting to us. These are our survival impulses. We use them to solve the challenges the muck factor poses in our lives.

The drives to fight, freeze, and run are found in all species, from insects and rodents to primates and human beings. Survival skills are thought to even predate the reptilian, or most primitive, brain. The primal mammalian brain and its rapid-fire survivalist response, found in all vertebrates for over 100,000,000 years, is part of our DNA programming. These three coping styles are an integral part of every one of us. Since these protectionist responses are primal, we are often unconscious of them going into action, especially when we feel threatened or perceive something as intimidating. This is true even if we are not consciously aware that we feel threatened.[xvii]

Understanding and managing the three protectors is an essential part of overcoming the boomerang effect, as their overuse perpetuates its cycle. Our emotional and mental triggers generate protectionist reactions. Things that emotionally threaten us—like feelings of imperfection, vulnerability, insecurity, fear, hurt, sadness, shame— and perceptions that threaten us—such as the belief that we are not good enough—set off the protectors' responses. This can cause many problems for us, as we often don't recognize or identify that we feel emotionally or mentally threatened, or we blame the world and others for our problems. If we become conscious of the threat, it is often only after the fact, when we've already reacted to it. For instance, we regularly don't realize what is making us insecure, anxious, or scared. Heck, most of the time our mind is so overactive, we know little of what is going on in there; and we often don't pay attention to our own emotions. We're too busy focusing on what the world and its inhabitants are doing to us, or criticizing ourselves for being stupid or not good enough.

Then there is the matter of denial. We deny what we perceive as negative—fear, hurt, sadness, vulnerability—and sugarcoat it as something prettier and more palatable to our minds. If we don't even know our emotions and don't pay attention to much of what we're thinking, or we take our perceptions at face value, believing them to be the truth, and don't challenge our beliefs, it will be hard for us to recognize the protectors. We may not realize, for instance, that we are acting in a controlling manner because we feel abandoned; that we are craving comfort food because we feel inadequate; that we are raging in our head about another's behavior because we feel insecure; or that we have labeled something as negative simply because we have learned to see the world and ourselves that way, not because it is actually so. Whether or not we are conscious of our emotional and mental threats, expectations, or belief systems will have no impact on the protectors' reactions. They don't require any awareness from us to fire off. Thus, we can feel anxious, angry, and depressed for reasons that are decidedly unclear. We can perceive that things are bad solely because that is the way we learned to view the world and ourselves.

Conditioning plays a role in making us unconscious of the protectors' presence. The mind and body are interconnected and bidirectional.[xviii] So we might not necessarily be aware of the external and internal triggers that activate the survival response, but the mind/body will know to react protectively to what it has learned to perceive or associate as threatening. Thus, if we've been frequently put down and experienced painful feelings of inadequacy as a result, we can become sensitive to criticism. We will then respond protectively to even the most benign association with put downs, such as reacting defensively to a stranger's probing glance, perceiving it as a criticism of what we're wearing.

What we perceive as threatening activates the autonomic nervous system, which involves the fight, freeze, and flight reactions. The brain forms a pattern, whereby something associated with fear will trigger other false signals based on past associations. As a result, we can be completely unaware of why we are anxious, scared, or depressed. Dr. Bruce Perry, an internationally renowned researcher on children's mental health and the neurosciences, offers this example of the unconscious aspect of the fear response. A young boy experienced severe abuse from his father. Two years after being removed from the situation, the child suffered a serious brain injury and for eight months was in a coma. Unconscious and nonverbal though he was, he would scream and moan, and his heart rate would increase dramatically, not just from his father's presence when he visited, but also from the sound of his voice via audiotapes and the smell of his clothes. Although the child's brain was not capable of conscious perception, he was still able to sense, process, and react, even though his brain's higher areas were damaged and incapable of full function.[xix]

As if all these things weren't enough, another reason we are challenged in being able to recognize our protective responses can be traced to the dominant organ located at the top of our skull: the brain. We use it to justify the need for the protectors' existence. This can greatly distort our perspective. For instance, we see the perceived threat or problem as coming from the outside world, and we label it as bad. We need to protect ourselves from what we view as terrible things and people. To do otherwise would be foolhardy and stupid. The world and its inhabitants, after all, can be suspect at best and downright damaging at worst. There's a lot of scary stuff in this random and unpredictable world that we inhabit, and we need to protect ourselves. The mind will decipher and analyze what that is based on past experiences and future projections. Then it will rationalize the legitimacy of the protective responses, allowing them to gain more power and dominance. So we rationalize getting angry at the idiot who did that ridiculous thing, justify not trying again after a failure, reason away eating the tub of ice cream after a bad day, defend our unwillingness to change.... The manners in which we can rationalize are indeed infinite.

HABITUAL AND INDISCRIMINATE USE

The bad news is that we invariably overuse our ingrained survival skills to resolve the conflict the muck factor poses.[xx] This perpetuates the boomerang effect, causing us to feel stuck and boxed into our stress and struggle. Overuse means that we habitually or indiscriminately manage our challenges through the protectors, be that for a specific circumstance (like avoidance patterns in relationships) or in general throughout life (like struggling too much with everything, everyone, and the self). *Habitual* use is defined by the routine practice of responding to difficulties and challenges—be they a specific thing, like a weight, relationship, or money issue, or general problems throughout the day—in the manner of the protectors. For instance, we keep ourselves overly busy and stressed to avoid aloneness, so can protect ourselves from the pain of loneliness, isolation, and emptiness. *Indiscriminate* use means that we use the protectors far too much, and generically apply their specific responses to the many different situations and people we encounter. We are unable to see the diversity of alternate responses that can be used to resolve the specific or general challenges we experience. We cannot recognize or even understand alternative ways to think, react, and behave. For instance, if we indiscriminately worry to protect ourselves from the possibility of something bad happening, it will be difficult to be calm in the face of challenges. We simply do not know how to, or cannot even perceive such a tranquil reality, though we may long for it.

The overuse of the protectors occurs not only because are we mostly unconscious of them and rationalize them, but it also feels natural to use the protective responses. We think like them—our internal dialogue—

when it comes to matters of perceived threat, be that threat big or small, significant or innocuous, conscious or unconscious. But their overuse only keeps the circle of mucks regurgitating, what I call the mucky-go-round. Like a mother's arms, the protectors are our comfort zone, our nurturers and caretakers. Their responses easily become habitual and indiscriminate, or generic behavioral patterns, and parts of our mentality and viewpoint. They are how we try to manage a world, humanity, and mind/body that is variable and capricious. When the protectors dominate, it feels as if they control us, instead of we them. We are confused about the things we do. The whys and wherefores elude us. It is common for us to examine these protective responses retrospectively, after the deed is done and we feel regretful, ashamed, guilty, or self-critical. Or we shirk responsibility, shifting blame onto others and the situations for making us feel and behave the ways we do. And so the circle stays the same, and we remain stuck in the muck of our stress, strain, and struggle.

The good news, however, is this: what makes us stand apart from other species is our ability to make choices about how we respond to our environment. We can become conscious of ourselves and self-directing. That's the power we have over the primitive survival skills. This allows us the opportunity to consciously train ourselves, so that we are aware of our fighting, hiding, and escapist impulses; especially when they are getting out of hand, as they are most apt to do in the area of perceived—consciously or not—threats. We can learn to recognize protectionist behavior, even if we do not immediately understand the root cause of the emotional triggers. Doing this opens up the door to healing, growth, fulfillment, and deeper personal or spiritual meaning. The way to break the protectionist stronghold is to address and modify its response by knowing the nature of the beast itself. Then we can backtrack to the source of the reaction, when we are clearer and calmer. So we take care of the trigger first, and sort out the cause later. The exercises and techniques to help you do that are provided in chapter 13.

You will be learning about the mindset of the protectionist responses in the upcoming chapters. This will help you become more aware and responsible for them. As they are largely unconscious within us, they are easily rationalized, overly dominant, habitual, and non-discriminating or discerning. Understanding the three protectionist personifications that I described in the previous chapters (chapters 2, 3, and 4) are the first of these steps to help you more clearly see yourself and your mentality, inner dialoguing, reactions, thoughts, and behaviors. You are on your way to liberating yourself from the trap of the boomerang effect and taking charge of your life.

THE MIRRORS

Let me explain more about the personifications that you met so far in this book: Mucky, Glade, and the Mi-mies: Mi-mi the Fighter, Mi-mi the Hider, and Mi-mi the Runner.

Who is Mucky?

Mucky is the face of the muck factor. In other words, if the muck factor were a person, he would be called Mucky. His personification represents what you perceive or experience as negative, unpleasant, distasteful, problematic, or hurtful: criticism, rejection, disrespect, humiliation, abandonment, shame, insecurity, fear, failure, instability, lack of accomplishment, put downs, loss, poverty, violation. The list is endless. Mucky is both within you and around you. He is a part of your own identity: the shadows, shames, imperfections, and hurts that you struggle with; the fragmented, limited, or damaged parts of your personality. Mucky is also the person or thing in your life that you view as unsavory.

Through the Mucky characterization, you will become more aware of your internal dialogue and perceptions, and will better understand yourself at a more unconscious level, which is a basis for creating change. You might find the Mucky characterization to be childlike and rudimentary at times. That is so for a reason. When we find ourselves facing stress and strife, our responses become more primitive and elementary. The characterization of Mucky is based on the way people depict their inner dialogue and personal struggles during their SIT sessions with me. Again, this characterization provides a mirror, allowing you to see your own internal dialogue, actions, and behaviors better.

Who is Glade?

I've also created a personification to portray the other side of the muck factor equation: all that is clear, light, bright, and positive. I call this personality Glade. The word *glade* may not be familiar to you. You may only be aware of it as an air-freshener product, so let me introduce the concept to you now. A glade is an open and bright space or clearing. It originates from the word *glad*, which of course means joy and happiness. In this book, the word *glade* is used to refer to positive feeling states, like contentment or confidence; or a place where light shines brightly, and peace and serenity reign. Glade, the character, personifies all that we perceive as good and positive: happiness, joy, contentment, confidence, peace, serenity, love, and harmony. Like Mucky, Glade is someone or something that you meet in your external world (such as the people and situations you view as positive), and also a part of your own identity, the part of you that you perceive as positive. The Glade characterization will help you gain deeper insight into what gets in the way of attaining or sustaining positives in your life, so that you can better hold onto the things that affirm and uplift you. Like Mucky, Glade has been fashioned from the way people depict their journey to find happiness during their SIT sessions with me.

Who is Mi-mi?

Finally, there is Mi-mi to connote the generic self. This personification mirrors you back to you, so you can see your internal dialogue and perceptions more clearly, and thereby gain greater self-awareness. In this book, the self is not singular. It has many aspects. We can be happy or sad, passive or aggressive, powerful or weak, and so on. That there are so many parts to who we are means that we can easily feel fragmented, confused, and conflicted. When facing a challenge, we oscillate between this thought and that emotion, flipping back and forth more times than we can count in a matter of minutes, unsure about who we are and what to choose, think, or feel. Our complexity adds to the conflicts we encounter.

From my experiential SIT work with my clients, I have come to view three particular parts of the self to be the most responsible for keeping us stuck in the boomerang effect. These are our primal reactions to the challenges we face: fighting, hiding, and running. Thus I create three different parts of the generic self in the form of Mi-mi: Mi-mi the Fighter, Mi-mi the Hider, and Mi-mi the Runner. These characterizations will help you see your internal dialogue, attitudes, and behaviors more clearly to gain deeper self-awareness. They will be interacting with the Mucky and Glade characterizations in vignettes as a way to awaken you to your mostly unconscious reactions and self-talk. Once again, you might find these characterizations childlike and rudimentary. Remember: when we are confronted with stress, strife, and strain, our responses become more disintegrated, primitive, and elementary. Our worldview narrows, blinding us to other possibilities and limiting our perspective. Hence, we end up more stuck than liberated. We become so self-absorbed and self-centered that it's all about the self—"What about *me*? Why is this happening to *me*? Why are they doing this to *me*?" our minds scream—and we forget the world that exists beyond the one we know and have become accustomed to accepting. We lose sight of our potential.

METAPHOR

Because of the limitations of language, I have to ascribe a sex to each character. I make the protectors female as they are Mi-mies, which is a female name. Hence, Mucky and Glade are male to balance this out. However, they can be any sex you want them to be. Feel free to improvise. I've created these unique terminologies, personifications, and metaphoric vignettes to help you, the reader, break out of limiting mental boxes, over-rationalizations, and preconceived or biased associations that could possibly get in the way of your understanding and growth. For instance, the devil is stereotypically perceived as malevolent, wicked, and evil; while an angel is typecast as goodness, saintliness, mercifulness, and peace. Mucky and Glade, although not necessarily neutral, don't have particularly strong cultural or idiomatic pigeonholes. These terms can assist you in stretching outside of the familiar or limited ways of thinking that can keep you stuck, and help you better understand why you operate in the world the way that you do.

Additionally, the visual nature of metaphor creates the opportunity for us to bypass the limitations of logics. It opens us up to the boundless vista of the imagination, where we can resource greater insight, understanding, or perspective. That is, we can see things differently. Mucky, for instance, may sound like a childlike term to some, but the playfulness of the name can open the mind to view what might usually be seen as bad or negative in a more neutral or less threatening way. The idiom can help to lighten the weight of our perceived load, and even add a chuckle to our day. Maybe things aren't as bad as they seem if they're just a muck. So next time you're having a bad moment—stuck in traffic, angry at a coworker's rudeness, irritated at a long line—remember: it's not such a big deal, it's just a muck. Perception can change "bad" into "not so bad."

RECAP OF KEY CONCEPTS

Glade: Personification of the glade. Glade represents all we perceive as being bright, good, and positive in life. These are things like happy feelings, optimistic thoughts, supportive relationships, uplifting situations, and wonderful experiences.

habitual use of the protectors: Habitual use is defined by the routine practice of responding to difficulties and challenges—be it a specific thing, like a weight, relationship, or money issue, or general problems throughout the day—in the manner of the protectors. For instance, we keep ourselves overly busy and stressed to avoid aloneness, so can protect ourselves from the pain of loneliness, isolation, and emptiness.

indiscriminate use of the protectors: Indiscriminate use is defined by our inability to see the difference between the many different kinds of responses, outside of the protectors' modus operandi, that we can have for the various challenging circumstances we encounter. We cannot see or even understand alternative ways to think, react, and behave. For instance, if we indiscriminately worry to protect ourselves from the possibility of something bad happening, it will be difficult to be calm in the face of challenges. We simply do not know how to do this, or cannot even perceive such a reality, though we may long for it.

Mi-mi: Pronounced me-me, connotes the self.

mirrors: Mucky, Glade, and the Mi-mies (Mi-mi the Fighter, Mi-mi the Hider, and Mi-mi the Runner) are personifications of mindsets and inner dialogues that allow you to see yourself more clearly.

Mucky: The muck factor's personification. It is the identity that the muck factor assumes. He represents all that we perceive as negative, challenging, and difficult in life. These are things like painful emotions, downbeat thoughts, challenging circumstances, painful memories, and miserable relationships.

protectionist responses: Fighting, hiding, and running; or better known as the fight, freeze, and flight reactions to perceived danger.

protectors: The personas of the three protectionist responses to fight, hide, and run.

glade: An open, clear, bright space or clearing. Glade originates from the word *glad*, which means joy and happiness. It is a place where light shines brightly, and peace and serenity reign. It is the opposite of a muck.

MUCKY

9: THE LITTLE PEOPLE IN YOUR HEAD

It may be said without hesitation that for man the most important stressors are emotional, especially those causing distress.... The stressor effects depend not so much upon what we do or what happens to us but on the way we take it.... As a rule a problem arises because we are conditioned or predisposed to react in a certain way when meeting the stressors of daily life.[xxi]

We now know that our protectionist responses to fight, freeze, and flight are part of the rudimentary DNA programmed into all species. Here's the problem: human beings are anything but rudimentary. We are complex creatures who live intricate emotional, mental, physical, and spiritual lives. These primitive responses cannot and do not successfully manage the enormity of our existence. Nonetheless, we chronically overuse them to our detriment, and even keep employing them when they are destroying the very thing we are trying to protect: our happiness, harmony, peace, and positive thoughts and emotions.

Why do we do continually fall back on the three primitive protectors? Why do common sense and reason not prevail when the protectors rear their prehistoric heads? The answer lies in the simplistic nature of protectionism. As it is primal, we don't have to learn it. It is inborn, preverbal, and precognitive. The protectors, then, are an integral and preeminent part of who we are. We come hardwired with the three protectors as nature's way of taking care of its own. They're our old-fashioned method, a precursor to thought processing. Thus, protectionist responses don't require "logical reason" and "critical, objective thinking." Instead, they are automatically activated when we perceive threats of all kinds: emotional, mental, physical, and spiritual. Their defense reactions are immediate. Nanoseconds, in fact. There is a surge of biochemical responses that instruct us to run, hide, or fight. The three protectors bypass what we label as rational thought processing.

The unsophisticated, infantile, and guileless use of the protectionist responses in early life form a significant part of our psychological, emotional, and physiological makeup. They become *habitual*, which translates into unconscious. Since we learn to habitually reason and emote in the manners of these primitive coping responses when managing our perceived stress, we mostly don't realize that we are using them. We go about our life interpreting the world and ourselves in their way, reacting from their perspective, reasoning in the manner of their worldview, without even being aware of the root of these thoughts, emotions, and rationalizations. It is just the way we are, what we think, what we feel, and what we do when we perceive threats of all kinds. These protectionist responses are used to safeguard our sense of self or identity. Identity consists of our body, mind, emotions, beliefs, culture, and anything else we consider to be who we are. Protecting the self is necessary to ensure our survival.

And this is the point where things get messy and chaotic. Because protectors are part of our identity—they are part of who we are, what we think and feel—we need to *protect them* as well. That is, we need to preserve their protectionism in order to ensure safety and control in our lives. That's right, our survival. This is what makes it difficult to challenge their overuse and dominance. Instead, we rationalize and justify their status and place in our lives, because we associate them with safekeeping and well-being, or survival. Therein lies the reason that they ensnare and entrap us, and hence, the boomerang effect. The irony: we end up needing to protect ourselves from our own protectors.

However, it is hard to see any of this when we perceive any kinds of threats, be they real or imaginary, conscious or unconscious. As the protectors give us the illusion of safety and control—a core need—we are seduced by them at every turn, and they draw us into their ever-enclosing web. They blind us and trap us in a shallow, limited box of illusion and distortion that robs us of our power and will. Instead of feeling in control, which is why we are continually seduced by them, they leave us feeling the opposite: out of control to direct our own emotions and thoughts. They become our thoughts and emotions, and unfortunately their primitive worldview is fear-based and negative. They are the parasite that takes over its host. Who's the boss now?

The fact that we protect our protectors creates a feedback loop, whereby the fear or threat becomes a self-fulfilling prophecy. That is, the negative expectation is fulfilled, though we won't easily see this. For instance, the more we try to protect ourselves from life's perceived negatives by worrying about them, the more negativity (not to mention anxiety and fear) we create, due to the excessive negative thinking that is the nature of worry. We worry as a means to prevent negativity from harming us, but the worry itself feeds negativity. Hence, the boomerang effect. Though we will often seem irrational and unreasonable to others when the protectors are in high gear, in the world of our fish bowl, we will feel quite the opposite—sensible, smart, practical, and realistic.

As you may now notice, overusing the protectors means that we are actually creating the very thing that we are trying to protect ourselves from. But since the three protectors are part of our inner dialogue, mindset, and emotional life, they function under the radar. We believe in them; we trust them. They are how we think, rationalize, emote, and make sense of the world; how we cope with the onerous, unpredictable muck factor. In this way, they easily overpower our good sense and reason and run amuck, unchecked and uncensored, creating chaos, madness, and mayhem. We need to be aware of their entrapment in order to take charge of our lives and direct our mind, emotions, and body along a more positive, empowering path.

HOMUNCULI

A homunculus is a fully formed, miniature human being. The three protectors work like homunculi inside our heads, with minds and thoughts of their own. They are a part of who we are and so subtly controlling, they function under the radar of our consciousness. We generally go about our daily activity with little awareness that *they* are moving *us* along with them, rather than we taking control of them. Ask yourself the following questions:

- Have you ever tried telling yourself to be calm, but panic or anger took over and you couldn't rein in these feelings no matter how you tried?
- Have you ever felt that your emotions were controlling you rather than you controlling them? That is, worry, fear, anxiety, insecurity, etc., were bigger than your ability to stop them, like the panic of public speaking?
- Has your mind ever been overactive and you couldn't quiet it? For instance, your mind is just busy, busy, busy, ruminating about your day, the bad thing that happened to you last year, money woes, relationship issues, work crises, weight issues … even though you are trying to shut off the mind?
- Have you ever tried to tell yourself positive things but couldn't shake the negativity? Or the negativity sneaks back in without you even realizing it?
- Have you ever delayed or put off a call you had to make to let someone down?
- Have you ever procrastinated about doing a boring chore and watched TV or played on the computer instead? You do this even though you know you're going to get into trouble with your boss, partner, roommate, or parent.

If you answered yes to even one of the questions above, you know what it feels like when the protectionist response takes over. Oftentimes, and far more frequently than our minds can possibly grasp, we don't recognize them for what they are. They feel so much a part of us that we naively and regularly refer to them as *being* who we are. While this is technically correct, it gives the protective—and thus primal—responses power over how we handle the muck factor. We relinquish responsibility and ownership for our life choices, and get trapped in the vicious circle of their boomerang effect. To grab a hold of our power, to take charge of our lives, we need to be conscious of these primal protectionist responses, since we tend to be unconscious of them. That is because we are so accustomed to seeing them as part of our identity: how we think, feel, and react.

Unique Brand of Logics

The protectionist responses have their own unique brand of logics that we are unaware of. An outside observer would call it irrational. Their focus is very narrow, centered singularly on safeguarding us from threat. They see and know nothing else. Their vision is impaired, their viewpoint often childlike and simple. So the world becomes discombobulated, distorted by their worldview of protectionism, control, and safety. They fool us into believing that they are the answer to our problems. They keep us safe, powerful, in control, and reasonable, rather than recognizing that at base we are vulnerable and afraid, and our existence is unpredictable. It is important to understand the unique logics of the three protectors, for they will easily trap and ensnare us without our awareness.

In the next three chapters, you will likely see different aspects of your protectionist nature in all of the protectors: Mi-mi the Fighter, Mi-mi the Hider, and Mi-mi the Runner. This is because they are *all* based upon avoiding, hiding, and controlling what you consciously or unconsciously perceive as threatening. So you will relate to Mi-mi the Runner, Mi-mi the Fighter, and Mi-mi the Hider. However, the three protectors are distinguished from one another by their *mindset*. Each one has its own worldview, or way of interpreting the muck factor that forms our internal dialogue. What you will be looking at here is how you habitually approach, process, and manage the threat of the muck factor and the problems it brings. It is the *way* that we employ our protectors and the *philosophy* behind their different defenses that distinguishes one from the other. This is all about the manner in which we cope with our challenges and seek rewards.

Keep this in mind, then, as you read: the protectors' responses are the ways that you react to a problem when faced with perceived stress and strife. Their positions are not to be confused with your attitudes and behaviors as you deal with situations that are not entrenched problems or random, non-specific events. For instance, fighting to get a specific job or education that you want is not the protectionist pattern of consistently fighting *with* a problem; such as struggling with your partner, wanting him/her to acknowledge you so that you can be validated. Running toward an opportunity—like a great sale, assuming you have sufficient funds—is not the protectionist impulse of running *from* the pain inside your heart by shopping too much. Hiding from the nosy neighbor or retreating to hear your own voice amidst the din of confusion is not the protectionist motivation to hide away from the world to safeguard yourself.

As you read their depictions in the next three chapters, try not to get caught up in pigeonholing yourself into a particularly protectionist category. Instead, focus your attention on understanding the seduction and trap of the three protectors. All of them will be inside you. One or two might stand out more. The goal is to see the ways they operate within you, so you can be much more aware of yourself and less drawn into the traps of their distortions and illusions. That is what I want you to take from their personality profile. It is certainly not my intention for them to become more of a box that contains you. Rather, they are a construct or context to help you understand yourself, your mindset, your feelings, and your internal dialogue better.

Additionally, the three protectors function as *hard* and *soft* protectors. Hard protectors are when the Fighter, the Hider, and the Runner in you are so set in protectionist mode, you cannot see other ways of approaching your challenges, be they real or imaginary. And with time and conditioning, what is real and what is imagined becomes blurry. It is more about what we perceive as the problem, rather than what is actually the problem.

Let's say, then, that you are accustomed to being in a relationship, bad though it is. In your mind, being alone is a bigger and more real threat than a bad relationship. It scares you to be alone, and you don't think you could manage that, never mind that you already feel alone most of the time in your relationship. The reality in your mind is that you are not alone. You are coupled. Unhappily, yes, but who's counting that? Additionally, since you spend so much time ruminating and complaining about your partner's bad behavior, your mind is well occupied. You have no time to feel alone; you're busy complaining about him or her as you "protect" yourself from loneliness. And so it is that you unwittingly dig yourself deeper and deeper into the quagmire, believing that you're doing the opposite: controlling the problem and attaining your reward.

Soft protectors, on the other hand, are when your protectionism is more flexible and allowing. The softer the protectors are, the easier it is to liberate ourselves from the boomerang effect and take charge of our lives.

UNLEARNING

Unlearning the protectionist responses is required for us to live conscious, healthy, and complete lives. To thrive, grow, and empower ourselves, we need to get past their seductions, distortions, and illusions. We are the only creatures in the animal kingdom with the types of complex brains that allow us to reason like we do. We have the ability to make conscious choices that override our survival impulses. Training our minds, hearts, emotions, and body *to be still* through the compulsion to run; *to let go* when we're driven to fight; and *to open* instead of hide, helps us to override the boomerang effect. But that is indeed a challenging task, because the three protectors are opposed to such thing as stillness, surrender, or openness in the face of any perceived threat. In fact, it is their job to do the exact opposite thing. As they operate at such an unconscious, habitual level, it is essential that you are more aware of their manner of distortion and safeguarding, so you can subdue their power and take charge of your own life.

The vignettes you will read in the next three chapters will help you get deeper into the mindset of the protectionist responses. Each personification describes the particular pattern of protectionist thinking, inner dialoguing, and behavior. This is not who you are all the time, but when the protectors kick in to "help" you manage what you consciously or unconsciously perceive as the muck factor. So apply the descriptions to how you deal with your perceptions of emotional challenges, imperfections, vulnerabilities, and threats, rather than to every part of your life. For instance, you may think of the protective way you dealt with heartache or a difficult professional situation. Also consider that there are soft and hard protective responses. Some situations make you more protectionist than others. In general, the more threatened, vulnerable, hurt, or imperfect you feel and the more that something matters, the greater the protectionist response. Always keep in mind: protectionist mentality is distorted thinking. Now I am going to hand over the mike to the three protectors: Mi-mi the Fighter, Mi-mi the Hider, and Mi-mi the Runner. They will help you understand more about how you function when their mindsets—their voices in your head—take over.

Recap of Key Concepts

hard protectors: Hard protectors are when the protectionist responses of fighting, hiding, and running are so dominant and rigid, we cannot see other ways to manage the stress, strain, and strife we encounter. We are stuck in the distortion and the box of their mentality.

soft protectors: Soft protectors are when the protectionist responses of fighting, hiding, and running are less dominant, allowing us to see others ways to manage the stress, strain, and strife we encounter. While they influence and seduce us, we have a perspective wider than their enticement.

GLADE

10: The Defender of Glade

"It should be."

My name is Mi-mi the Fighter. I am the defender of what I perceive to be Glade, which is anything that makes me feel good. The need to control and conquer my perception of bad or negative things—Mucky—is tantamount to my existence. It defines who I am and what I do. It is my reason for being. Control is how I protect myself against the challenges of the capricious muck factor: the hurts, fears, stresses, and problems. What I am trying to do is keep my concept of Glade around. Holding Mucky at bay is how I accomplish this. So if freedom is my notion of Glade because it makes me feel so very good, I will fight anything that threatens to take that away. Whatever I view as trying to rob me of my perceived freedom, I will see it as Mucky, no matter that it might actually be good for me, like responsibility, security, commitment, and discipline. They don't feel as good, so that makes them Mucky to me. That is how distortions easily occur in my world of Mi-mi the Fighter.

Struggling is my only way. I never think outside of this box, and I don't look for other approaches to manage the muck factor. Mi-mi the Fighter is who I am. This is my role and purpose in life, and I take my job very seriously. I'm alert and ready 24/7 to rise to the occasion of conquering what I perceive as Mucky; and yes, this perception is subjective, based on my past experiences and interpretations, learning, conditioning, and environment. I never know when Mucky will rear his ugly head, so I always need to be prepared to fight. That does keep me overly anxious and worried, but I'm alert. And that's all I care about being. In fact, that's my job description. I'm just filling its requirements.

My humble beginnings will make you better understand this fighter in me. When I was a child, there were times when I felt abandoned and frightened. I felt like I was alone, with no one in the world. I had to fend for myself. I wanted to be free from the bad things that were happening to me. I needed to protect myself from the hurt, but I had no foundation. My trust and belief in life were tenuous. I did not feel worthy at times, and I believed that it was my fault that my parents weren't able to give me what I needed. It felt like I was in quicksand, stuck and immobilized. I wanted to be free from this. So I pretended to be strong to help me cope, and anger worked. It liberated me from my sense of powerlessness. Although I felt the hangdog, the anger inside was powerful. When things were bad for me, I didn't think life was fair. I coped with the hard world outside me by making it hard inside of me as well. Then I wouldn't have to feel the pain. I came to believe that I was the only one I could ever rely on. That was the beginning of the scrapper in me.

I learned to associate fighting with control, power, and freedom. I used it to get what I wanted. That was its great reward in situations where I otherwise would have been helpless and trapped. It's because of the Fighter in me that I was able to survive the mucks of my life. At least, that's how I viewed it. The evolution of this is that now I don't always know when to put my arms down and surrender when my vulnerabilities are triggered, or when my protectors are really hard. I lose perspective. I am convinced that I can somehow control and overcome what I perceive as Mucky, if I just keep pushing and shoving.

Let's say, then, that I'm fighting to protect my Glade of freedom. I will see even the most innocuous thing as taking that away, like time constraints or my partner's needs. I start fighting against the things and people that I view as trying to control me. Even when I actually need boundaries, because I am becoming irresponsible, I will not want to surrender my Glade of freedom. That is how my distortions can turn on me and damage positive things—like relationships—in my quest for my ideal of what is good.

Although I might leave a particularly bad circumstance, my fighter mentality will keep me struggling inside myself, arguing in my head with the image of the person I see as mucking me up. Or I replay the negative scenario in my mind, beating myself up about how I could have acted differently. It's hard for me to just let go or walk away from a perceived problem, even if I extract myself physically from the situation. My mind will still be running amuck, recycling the drama, invested in its goal to conquer the obstacle. I will be preoccupied with my idea of how it should be and want to fight for that. It's hard for me to accept that I cannot overcome a difficulty; and I will either blame everything outside of me for Mucky's presence, or blame myself. The need for control will get out of control, creating a backlash of muckiness. For instance, in my quest to control anything getting in the way of my freedom, I am irresponsible, reckless, and decidedly out of control. The struggle will define me, and peace will become a theory that I read about in a book. And so it is that I ride the mucky-go-round of beasts and monsters, seeking a Glade that is nowhere to be found. Ironic, isn't it, for I am supposed to be Glade's defender.

Despite the outer bravado that being Glade's defender might provide, do not be fooled. I am absolutely *terrified* of what I perceive Mucky to be. This can be anything: fear of commitment, fear of abandonment, fear of rejection, fear of being consumed, fear of not being good enough, fear of pressure.... There are just so many things that I can be frightened of. Most of the time, I am not aware of these fears. After all, I'm trying to protect myself from these things by controlling or fighting against them. So no, I won't be claiming fear. But it is what lies beneath my role of Fighter. It's hard for me to admit that I'm scared anyway. I dislike the vulnerability and humility. It goes against my grain. I couch my response in terms like, "Hey, I'm just standing up for myself," or, "Look, I need to protect myself from this crap," rather than admit that I'm just plain scared of what I perceive as Mucky. And of course, there is the standard denial, "Scared? What are you talking about? I'm scared of nothing!" But let me set the record straight: a defense only exists because there is an underlying fear. If you feel the need to protect, a fear is *always* beneath it.

When I am really steeped in denial, I do not recognize that my reactions stem from fear. Instead, I just blame the other person, the situation, or myself as the reason I'm mucked up—like when I feel worthless or not good enough. If I see the problem as something that is flawed or imperfect within me, I deal with these by beating myself up. So if someone puts me down, and I believe their criticism, and my inadequacy is triggered, I will beat myself up for not being good enough and causing the bad thing to happen, loser that I am. If I see the issue as being caused by something negative in my environment, I attack or struggle with those around me. Maybe not to their face, but certainly in my head. So that person who put me down will be enemy number one. I tell myself that I'm taking care of the problem in this way. Otherwise, everything will just get right out of hand.

Lest you get the impression that being Mi-mi the Fighter is all about belligerence, let me quickly correct that misapprehension. I can be equally passive and compliant. Remember, I want to *defend* the presence of what I perceive as Glade, even when I find it difficult to attain. I believe this is called passive-aggressive. When I am like that, I may look like I am "taking it," but I'm not giving in. I'm still focused on what should be. I'm not fighting with what's around me, but I sure am struggling inside of me. Or I'm biding my time. I'm keeping the peace, so to speak, but I am not surrendering. I think I'm right; things should be the way I want. Sometimes others can tell that too. I'll be nice, but I'll have attitude. This lets them know I'm not actually backing down. I will surrender when I feel beaten, but all the while I will be plotting for a way to conquer what I consider to be Mucky. So, if I surrender to another's needs, just to keep the peace, but am in the habit of protecting my sense of freedom and the right to do what I want, I will feel controlled. I will then act out my resentment in indirect ways, like arriving late for an event or leaving it prematurely.

When I am entrenched in the mindset of Mi-mi the Fighter—when I'm missing the fact that I am sinking deeper and deeper into a quagmire—I really believe that if I just keep going, I can eventually defeat what I perceive as Mucky. That if I just stick with it, I will make things different and conquer the problem. I will make them what they should be. Although the anger, resentment, chaos, and drama will be mucking me up, I won't see them as the problem. No, they are the solution. I am deluded by how comfortable I have become in my protectionist pattern and behavior. So when protecting my perception of freedom, for instance, I will not see my increasing irresponsibility as the issue, but the solution. What I perceive as another's control will further justify my behavior.

Being Mi-mi the Fighter can get me into big trouble, because I don't know when to give up, surrender, or walk away. That is like running to me, and even though I fantasize about doing so or I threaten to, I end up being pulled back into the struggle. I want an answer. I need to know why and how. I want things my way, the way they should be. This can manifest as me struggling with my emotions or thoughts, like guilt, shame, anger, resentment. Or I can be battling with the situation or person whom I see as causing the conflict. Often it is a combination of an internal and external struggle. Even when the struggling gets messy, such as when my battle to hold onto freedom is damaging my relationship, it is difficult for me to capitulate. I find ways to rationalize the struggle again. I have a hard time telling the difference between what I need to fight for and what I need to let go of. It gets to be one big blur. I don't realize how much the battle itself is the problem, so wrapped up am I in the struggle. I feel completely justified in fighting. This is how I end up defending what I consider to be Mucky, all the while thinking that I am protecting what I perceive to be Glade. Protecting my Glade of freedom, for instance, might muck me up because of all the reckless choices I make, but I can rationalize it in terms of fighting against a perceived threat to my liberty. "I should have this right," I will argue.

When fighting my idea of Mucky proves unsuccessful, it feels like a dark day in my world. Getting humbled is the worst experience for me. My pride is damaged. I feel like a loser and beat myself up about it—"Why didn't you try harder? What else could you have done? I thought you were smarter than this." I'll keep wondering what I should have or could have done, or what I didn't do right. I'll somehow forget or deny the weight and horror of the negativity that enclosed me. It won't matter that others are telling me I fought enough. Conversely, I will feel victimized and be angry at the world for defeating me.

This belief that my continual fighting can change or control what I perceive to be Mucky is what distinguishes me as Mi-mi the Fighter. It's all about what should be. I don't like to give in or give up that easily when it comes to the muck factor. I can appear to be quiet and demure, and yet still be focusing on how I can overcome my version of Mucky. I can feel defeated, tired, even believe that nothing will change and that I won't win, but I find surrender hard and humiliating. Fighting and controlling can become so much a part of me that I just don't know how else to be. The Fighter that I am is more comfortable being in conflict than being calm or peaceful. So I fall back into it whenever I feel vulnerable or threatened. That's how my world gets to be more like Mucky than Glade.

When I am really sold on my fighting mode—hard protectionism—I'll keep struggling with what I perceive to be Mucky, whether it is in my own head or with another thing or person. It is like I *need* to battle with Mucky. I want the control. I want to win. Everything should be the way I want. It feels unnatural to be passive, to *not* be waging some kind of combat. Struggling feels normal, the way that life is and the way that I am. That is how strong and overpowering the drive for control is. I find letting go really hard to do when I am like that. I lose all perspective. I get lost in the struggle. I push everything and everyone away so that I can maintain control. I dislike the weakness of my emotions. Surrender and humility feel so pathetic. Even though giving up control is difficult for all three of us protectors, it is especially challenging for me as Mi-mi the Fighter.

These are the reasons that I get really stuck in my circle of stress, strain, and struggle. I don't know when to walk away or to accept that I need to stop fighting in the face of vulnerability, imperfections, limitations, and perceived threat. Instead, I chip away to the point of exhaustion, not recognizing when it's time to just let go. In my hardest protectionist form, I am stubborn, implacable, and unwavering, even volatile and dangerous. When the protection gets hard-lined, I lose the ability to rationalize outside its narrow walls. It calls me to it, and like a sheep, I follow its pull all the way to the firing squad. When my protectionism is softer—that is, more balanced and flexible—I will eventually surrender, but I will still be testy about it, and easily pulled back into the struggle. I have to work hard and be disciplined, so as to not get drawn in.

General characteristics of Mi-mi the Fighter:

Soft Fighting: Challenging, demanding, testy, defiant, rebellious, insolent, audacious, foolhardy, rash, impulsive, disrespectful, know-it-all, headstrong.

Hard Fighting: Stubborn, unreasonable, pushy, belligerent, aggressive, unstoppable, threatening, destructive, manipulative, pugilistic, reckless, sabotaging.

11: The Keeper of Glade

"What if ...?"

My name is Mi-mi the Hider, and I am the keeper of what I perceive to be Glade. Glade is all the things that make me feel good in life. Hiding comes from the instinct to ward off danger. I camouflage myself so I don't get noticed; I stay motionless so that I cannot be seen. I am the chameleon that changes colors to blend into my fluctuating environment in order to control, to avoid, and to protect myself from my perception of Mucky. This is the mask I wear. The more invisible I am, the safer I will be, and the more Glade is protected. That is the world according to Mi-mi the Hider. It is the art of wallowing.

Let's say, for instance, that validation is my Glade. I just love when I get positive feedback and affirmation. That makes me feel good about myself: valued, worthy, important, secure. But when I experience negative responses, or interpret something as negative, that's Mucky in the house. I feel myself withering and retreating into a corner, where I wallow in inadequacy. All the while I mask it with the veneer of being cool and okay, perhaps by acting overly friendly. Can't let the world see I'm falling apart and get attacked more. The less I'm "seen," the less likely that others can make me feel bad about myself. So why put myself out there to get knocked down again? Only a fool does that.

Let me tell you how I got to be this way. When I was a young child, I learned to lock myself away so I wouldn't have to deal with the vulnerabilities of my life. Rejection and disapproval from others hurt me. I received negative messages about myself, at school and at home, that I wasn't good enough unless I followed the rules. I learned that love was conditional. I worked hard to excel so that I wouldn't experience disapproval. I loved the validation I received when I did well. Hiding behind the mask that others required me to assume—to be quiet rather than expressive, to please instead of disappoint by being what others wanted me to be—ensured approval. Validation felt so much better than dismissal; it was a Glade for me. So hiding behind the mask of perfectionism meant that I didn't have to feel I wasn't good enough. I became the chameleon. I got positive affirmation by being and doing what was demanded of me. Never mind that it cost me important parts of my identity and truth, that it didn't prepare me to handle what I perceived as failure. Although hiding made me feel fragmented and inauthentic, being liked was a whole lot better than rejection and disapproval.

When the world around me felt scary, especially when I was faced with my imperfections, I didn't know how to cope without feeling inadequate. Hiding behind control protected me from this. If I did everything right, no one would notice my flaws and the negatives couldn't reach me. Then no one and nothing could put me down, make me feel bad about myself, or hurt me. Hiding also helped numb my emotions. If I didn't feel too much, I wouldn't feel so bad about myself. By preventing the negatives from getting in, hiding protected my Glade of approval. I believed that it helped me hold onto any positive sense of self that I had. The feeling of safety that hiding gave me prevented me from breaking free of its barriers. I kept returning to my place of retreat whenever Mucky the Disapproving reared his ugly head. It was my comfort zone. Thus, hiding has become a part of me and how I deal with what I perceive to be the muck factor. Therein is the making of this Hider.

In my mind, hiding is what helped me survive the painful experiences that made me feel bad about myself, or bothered or hurt me in some way. Retreating helps me not to feel the wounds. It keeps everything and everyone at bay. Nothing can get close to me. I can shut down. I like the control that I believe this gives me. The downside of hiding, though, is that it is passive, and I get resigned to my problems. My thinking is all about, what if something bad happens again. I believe that Mucky will always come back to hurt or bother me, and I am powerless to stop it. That's why hiding is so necessary. I need a safe place where I can't be affected by the outside world, which I see as dangerous and precarious.

Let's say someone makes a negative comment to me after I volunteered to present at a meeting. I feel so bad about myself that I hide so I won't be exposed to criticism again. I see the world as the problem, not my inadequacy. But by hiding, I also sabotage all possibilities of moving forward in my life. I don't overcome the inadequacy, and it rules me. So I end up stuck in my world of inadequacy. Although I think I am getting away from the problem, I'm actually hiding in it. Still, hiding is a world of shadows that covers me in a protective blanket. It numbs and masks me, and this sense of safety makes me feel better and is my version of Glade. This is my brand of logics. I don't notice that I am becoming a shadow of myself as I hide in a dark world where I cannot be seen. It's not long before this darkness overpowers me, and I end up being in the same place I am trying to avoid: Mucky. I find myself wallowing in the very thing I'm trying to hide from.

As a lizard is green in a verdant environment and brown on a tree trunk to hide itself, I too mask and shift to protect myself from exposure to the precarious world, where people or things can make me feel bad about myself. I lose my sense of self in the process and wonder who I am. Where do I begin and the world end? I come to so strongly identify with the persona that I've adopted—like being nice or strong all the time—that I lose sight of who or what I feel is truly me. My boundaries get blurred. What was meant to protect me closes in on me. I am lost, alone, and confused, trying to sort out my own truth. Who am I? That's how hiding ends up mucking me up. It keeps Glade far away instead of protecting me from Mucky. For example, when I'm wearing my mask of perfectionism, I set up expectations that I can always be on and in control. Then I resent people for asking or expecting too much of me. I feel pressured to do everything right and gain approval. I am so afraid to disappoint, because that just makes me feel bad about myself, so I overcompensate. What if I make a mistake? Round and round and round I go, trapped in a cycle of perfectionism that gives me more grief than rewards. But hiding behind my perfectionism is the mask I wear to cover my insecurity.

Although I become a shadow of myself, it's hard for me to stop hiding. How else can I defend myself against the very real muck factor? Life is precarious and scary; people can be mean and critical. What if these bad things happen again? The less I show you who I am, the safer I will be. Exposure is threatening and anxiety-provoking for me. I prefer not to put my true self out there and reveal who I am, lest I get knocked down. Invisibility is safer. Otherwise, Mucky might see who I am and grab hold of me. I realize that this is contradictory. By disguising myself, I get all mucked up; but I don't see that when my focus is on safety. My perspective gets distorted. I think that my camouflage *protects* Mucky from destroying what lies beneath the mask. If he can't see it, he can't hurt it or ruin it. In that way, I believe that I keep Glade safe.

Let's say, then, that I am hiding behind my mask of perfectionism. I am afraid that if people see my inadequacies, they will tear me down and make me feel like I'm a loser. Again, the hiding doesn't make me see that the inadequacy is the root of the problem. I only focus on the people who I see as causing the problem, not understanding that they are only triggering my insecurities. Oh, what a mucky-go-round, because I am not even remotely perfect, and no matter how I try to hide, my limitations must surface. So the mask isn't safeguarding me. Additionally, the more perfect I try to be, the more pressured, panicked, and stressed I feel, so the more likely I am to mess up. What a boomerang.

My reason for hiding is all about what the big, bad mucky world and its inhabitants are doing to me. I am a victim, powerless and weak. "He abandoned me; they put me down; she was mean," is what I think. And, "What if it happens again?" Perceiving myself as a victim certainly mucks me up more. But the illusion of control that I get from hiding is what seduces me back to it. Although I blame the world for mucking me up, I also turn the finger back on myself. "It's all my fault, because I'm just not good enough. This proves it more. What if I mess up again?" the brain will chatter. "All the more reason to hide then, and not expose my weaknesses to the world, which will ostracize me for being so inadequate." And so the boomerang returns to its place of origin.

The irony with hiding is that it makes me more inclined to put up with the muck factor, although it's supposed to do the opposite. The longer I hide, the more mucked up I feel, and the more stuck I become.

Life becomes lackluster and austere. There is no light or joy. Everything is shut out and distant, and I lose sight of the other possibilities that exist. Hiding closes in on me, and Glade disappears. But I feel I'm safe, because I don't have to venture out into the world. That sense of safety is what my reward, or Glade, is. I stick to the muck that I know and that I can negotiate. That is my mindset. This, I believe, will keep that ever-elusive Glade with me. That is also how I get comfortable in the quagmire of my life. Twisted like a sour lemon, that's what this thinking is.

Let's say, once again, that I am hiding behind my mask of perfectionism, which creates pressure, stress, and anxiety in my life. The perfectionism doesn't change my inadequacies, which I continue to wrestle with. Actually, the quest for perfectionism highlights my ineptness, exacerbating the problem. So why not just take off that perfectionist mask, since hiding behind it is proving to be more of a problem than a solution? *What?* Are you kidding me? Then I have to expose and acknowledge my vulnerability. Then I don't get the reward I believe I get when I am able to be "perfect." All I'm left with is my inadequacy. At least perfectionism grants me some approval and validation. On and on my mind will go, finding new ways to justify the pattern that is causing my suffering, but I won't see it that way. It is my protection, not my pain.

When I am steeped in my hiding mode, I will not expect more from the world than what already exists as my life, like being dismissed, abandoned, or put down. I resign myself: that's just the way it is. I think this helps me better manage my difficult circumstances. If I don't expect or want or desire more, if I'm not willing to risk, I am protected from disappointment and hurt, and all the other things that scare me. I don't want to feel happy, in case sadness comes along again to muck me up, for instance. I don't notice the pessimism messing me up. I don't quite grasp that I am keeping out all that is Glade in order to protect me from what I perceive to be Mucky. Even when I can see this, I'm able to rationalize the need to sustain the behavior. Bad as it may be, it would be worse to do otherwise. I am safe, remember. Safe. My focus on safety and control to protect me from a world that is random and uncertain distorts my perspective. Resignation sets in. Mucky is just the way it is, what it is, and I have to take it. I can't expect more or better. I guess you can see how managing the muck factor in this way can get me really, really stuck. It only compounds negativity, fear, and darkness. Instead of being in control, I am powerless.

When I'm really deep in the hiding mode, it feels difficult to lift my feet from the floor. Frozen on the spot, I suffer a sense of sensory deprivation. Time moves slowly, and it's almost like I've been there forever. The more I move or struggle, the more frustrated I get because there is no reprieve. The muck factor has taken over my inner world to the point where it is claustrophobic, and I can't breathe. My mind is fixated on all the potential negatives that could occur. What if the plane crashes? What if the terrorists attack? But despite the drudgery, leaving is scarier than staying. I believe that without the protection of hiding from a world that is so unpredictable, there will be no Glade of safety. The control of perfectionism, for instance, is better than the vulnerability of inadequacy. Exposure and opening are the worst threats of all. So I stay in my shadow even if it's closing in on me. It is a self-defeating system. Not only does it not work, it fuels the problem, keeping out the positives. The result: numb, frozen, and stuck, not knowing who I truly am.

Let's say, then, that hiding behind my mask of perfectionism controls me more than I control it. I've gotten lost in the hiding. Anxiety and pressure take over, making me feel more and more inadequate. I lose sight of all other possibilities, so caught up am I in this role. The hiding stops me from surrendering the mask of perfectionism and risking criticism. I get stuck in the world I know, since I perceive it as safer than the precarious, unknown—and hence uncontrollable—world and its equally capricious inhabitants. The hiding makes me so closed off that other ways seem impossible. I say things like, "I don't know how ..." as in, "I don't know how to take off this mask I've worn for so long."

When I am in my hardest mode, I will hide behind my camouflage, hopeless, resigned, depressed, anxious, defeated, victimized, and powerless. I am very negative and pessimistic. I will give up, seeing no possible way out. My world is dark, dreary, and enclosed. When I am softer, I will stoically work with my difficult circumstances, but it requires that I work hard to not get drawn back into the loop of hiding. However, I will not easily recognize when other possibilities are available to me, so set am I on keeping myself safe rather than risking the unknown world.

General characteristics of Mi-mi the Hider:

Soft Hiding: Stoic, compliant, passive, predictable, safe, withdrawn, detached, distant, long suffering, disingenuous, insincere, unavailable, closed, timid, voiceless.

Hard Hiding: Powerless, hopeless, incapable, complacent, resigned, defeated, pessimistic, unreadable, unknowable, deceptive, absent, victimized, fake, pretentious, cold, inauthentic.

12: THE SEEKER OF GLADE

"If only ..."

My name is Mi-mi the Runner. I am the seeker of what I perceive as Glade, which are the things that reward me. I'm motivated to run from what I view as Mucky in my life, because I want to hold onto what makes me feel good. Escapism means that I don't have to deal with situations and people that make me feel bad about life and myself, like isolation. I want to avoid that stuff as much as possible. I have the underlying fear that the capricious Mucky will get into my world and push the equally uncertain Glade aside. Avoidance is much better for me than dealing with the negative stuff that brings me down. The control, power, and relief I get from escaping Mucky keep me running. Life is so much safer that way. Let's say, for instance, that I have a fear of isolation. The desolation, alienation, and vulnerability that it brings are terrible feelings. I'll do anything to escape it—staying in bad relationships, shopping too much, excess busyness. Anything is better than the horrible feeling of isolation.

This pattern of escapism began developing a long time ago. When I was a child, there were times when I felt alone, isolated, and misunderstood. My parents separated and had less time for me. I didn't feel important, and there wasn't a whole lot of security. It's not that I wasn't loved, just that things became more haphazard and chaotic. I started feeling different from everyone else. I didn't always fit in or feel valued. I felt lost in my own home, separate and apart. My sense of worth diminished. So I painted a pretty world that I could escape to, where I didn't have to deal with the things that bothered or hurt me. It made me feel better to imagine that everything was okay, to get as far away as I could from stresses, like isolation, that I didn't want to feel. Escapism became the way to manage the muck factor. Escapism meant that I didn't have to feel my pain, sadness, or hurt. I could be better, happier. That seduction was very compelling. And so here I am now, Mi-mi the Runner.

Being Mi-mi the Runner is a dynamic protectionist strategy based on my desire to find the silver lining. Why be with Mucky when I can have Glade? That's my mentality. My yearning to get away from what I perceive as negative keeps me thinking in terms of continually seeking more of the goodies in life. "If only" is the fuel that drives me. I am focused on how to make sure these negatives aren't allowed in to destroy the day. Escapism is about getting away from whatever brings me down, even just a little bit—boring laundry, tedious conversation, disappointing someone, heartaches, fear—so that I don't have to give up pleasure or peace. The problem is that Mucky always sneaks into my life with a disappointment here, a rejection there, getting in the way. So I forever have to be on the run, or Mucky is going to catch up with me. That's the circular track that I tread as Mi-mi the Runner. Round and round and round on the same mucky-go-round.

Running is the practice of being distracted in the world. Let's say I feel isolated and alone. I avoid these discomforts by finding other things to occupy myself to make me feel better: I go shopping, eat cake, get inebriated, watch too much TV. I ignore the problem so I don't have to deal with it. I continually abandon myself in this way. Not dealing with my stuff means that I need to run from myself over and over again. If only I could be happier …

Escapism makes it hard, often impossible, for me to be in the moment. It's difficult for me to be still. My mentality is always about being somewhere other than where I am when it comes to dealing with the muck factor. In my Runner's mind, there is always more, bigger, and better. "If only I could lose weight, make more money, find the right mate." I think in terms of "when"—when I have the money that will make me feel secure; when I meet the person of my dreams, so that I don't have to feel lonely; when I get a better job that will fulfill me; when I lose weight, so that I can feel good about myself. When I get to wherever it is that I imagine will help me escape the stress and struggle that is in my world, everything will be fine and paradise will be mine. If only ... So I'm busy running to get to the destination that I perceive to be Glade. For Mi-mi the Runner, it is not about the journey, only the end result and reward. I lose sight that the willy-nilly nature of Mucky means that he will always come back around, in some form or manner—as loneliness, stress, frustration, insecurity, and so on. I forget that everything comes with a price. Even if I get the person, the job, or the riches of my dreams, it will come with its own brand of challenges. When that happens, I will think about escaping that too.

Escapism, then, ends up being a problem in itself. I'll never get to where I'm seeking, because it simply doesn't exist. *If only* never materializes. But I sure like the high of getting away or flying off into the land of my own escapist making, where everything is "great" and "wonderful," and everyone is "good" and "loving." I'm blind and can't see clearly, but that's what escapism does to you. Let's say, then, that I'm avoiding the perceived misery of isolation. I will try to fill up my life with things that rescue me from it. I go from one situation or person to another, trying to find connection and attachment. I think that somewhere out there is the solution to the answer, that someone or something will save me. The first glimpse of salvation, I jump on it. Maybe it's the gossiping friend that I hang out with because we agree the moon is round, but who ends up backstabbing me. But I'm onto the next, in search of my opportunity to be saved, without looking at myself long enough to learn the lessons that experiences can teach me. Of course not. I just want to be rescued. If only ...

Always wanting to be somewhere that's better than where I am ends up mucking me up. I feel disgruntled with my life. I don't appreciate or see the positives that actually exist. The muck factor gets in the way with things like disappointments, problems, and hurts. My escapist mentality means that I spend my time focusing on these negatives to keep me aware of them, given that they are so unpredictable. Better to fixate on problems so I can be alert and ready to get away from them. But this negative thinking, in turn, keeps me stuck in the muck as my attention is focused on the inimicable. Being on high alert for negatives in order to escape them, means that I don't notice enough of what is good in my life. My mind is too much on the darkness or dangers in the world and the imperfections in me.

That is how I work against myself. I never feel like I attain what I desire, mostly because my running prevents me from seeing, feeling, or cherishing anything. So caught up am I in getting away from what is or could potentially be Mucky, I don't hold onto Glade. Indeed, I don't even have a barometer for what this fantastical thing called Glade actually is, because nothing's ever enough for long. Things and people don't ever stay all pretty and perfect. Escapism leaves me fearfully watching my back for problems, wondering when Mucky will turn up. I distrust what is good, for the muck factor always returns like a boomerang. I don't see that my worries and fears push the good away. How can I really see anything? I'm so busy running, nothing is clear.

Let's say, for instance, that I connect with someone. I will feel good about it until a negative issue arises. Then I'm ready to bolt, thinking that something better must be out there. In that way, I stay alone. Never living in the moment means that I'm busy focusing on what mucks are present so I can get away from them. I look for and focus on bad things, like hurt or rejection. That way I can prepare myself to run, just in case. It also means that I project possible problems into the future—that this person could control me like the last person I dated—whether they actually exist or not. I create all kinds of illusionary scenarios that justify my avoidance and perpetuate the running. This stops me from taking risks that could liberate me from Mucky. I sabotage the good that is there by looking for the bad.

I also do the opposite. Instead of being blind to the positives, I ignore or deny the problems and indiscriminately focus on the good things. This gets me into a lot of trouble, because I make some pretty dumb choices. Like denying a lover's coldness, lying to myself that he or she is just preoccupied, so I can escape the desolation of isolation. I sugarcoat problems so that I can escape their fallout. Hence, I'd rather pretend that Mucky the Liar is just forgetful, rather than face being alone, given my fear of isolation. So either I'm all mucked up anticipating and thwarting Mucky; or I am steeped in so much denial that I'm stuck in terrible situations, pretending it's all good. As you can tell, my vision as Mi-mi the Runner is skewed and distorted through the lens of escapism. After all, I need to justify my behavior. Reality through my eyes is never very clear.

Imagine my life like this: there I am in the glade happily picking flowers. The place is beautiful. There is a pond, and everything is peaceful and calm. Inhaling the fragrant freshness around me, I feel connected to my surroundings, filled with the sense of completeness that is here. But then suddenly, out of nowhere, my mind wanders in the direction of Mucky, and it hits me that I am all alone and no one is there but me. I start thinking about experiences of isolation that have hurt me. I wonder if things will ever change. My mind starts spinning its desolate tales. If only I could meet someone wonderful. I get so caught up in the worry that I stop noticing where I am in the present moment, stop seeing the beauty that surrounds me. I'm anxious and afraid that I'll forever be alone; and then I am angry and resentful that my life is like this. Because of this anxiety, I lose the calm and sense of connection. The once beautiful place has become threatening. Now I need to get away from it, because I see it as the problem. It is making me feel isolated and abandoned. If only I could feel complete.

This is how I avoid myself. Either I blame something else for the problem, or I blame myself. If I decide the fault is everything and everyone else, I need to escape to somewhere else to make me feel better. By dumping the responsibility for all that is going wrong on whatever is around me, I end up seeking what I perceive as Glade outside of me. I want to be rescued from my pain. Thus, I look for someone to fill the holes in my soul. If I point the finger at myself, it makes me feel so bad about myself and overwhelmed, that all I want to do is feel better and get away from myself. So I distract myself with feel-good things, like food, partying, busyness, or relationship hopping.

But no matter where I point the finger, the truth is that I don't feel good inside myself. Even when I take ownership of my issue, I don't know what to do with it, given that I am so in the habit of wanting to get away from the muck factor. I just don't know how else to be. So I compartmentalize myself. A part of me is light and positive, and a part of me is imperfect and messy, and ne'er the twain shall meet. Then I can run to the parts of me that are secure, and deny or ignore the parts that are mucked up. What I perceive as positive is, of course, favored and adored: my strength, my kindness, my joie de vivre, for instance. My imperfections and vulnerabilities, on the other hand, like my insecurities, hurts, and fears, are pushed to the side so that I can get away from them. But the catch is that they are still there inside me. So Mucky is never far away, bubbling beneath the surface, threatening to erupt. I find myself stuck in the muck when I am working so hard to get away. More insidiously, my emotions and thoughts are precarious and all over the place. I never know when they'll erupt and mess with me, so I need to stay as far away from myself as possible to prevent that from happening.

When I cannot physically leave, my safety is the *belief* that I can some day or somehow get away from what is mucking me up. Denial and ignorance become my best friends. I drift off daydreaming about Glade. If only I could be rescued. If only Prince or Princess Charming would come get me. Escapism like this stops me from improving or recognizing the things that can get better. So where am I running to? The same situation recycles itself like a boomerang—the same insecurities and emotionally abandoning partners.

When running becomes a hard protection, I will indiscriminately want to leave. I will look to small, insignificant things to justify my running. I will not see that they can be resolved, so threatened am I by the mere possibility of the unpredictable Mucky taking over. I will not know when to stay put or fight through the challenge. The first signs of the muck factor—real or imagined, and most the time I don't know the difference—will make me want to get away, rather than be still and resolve conflict, whether the conflict is within myself or with other things or people around me. Nothing ever changes, because I do not stay put long enough to deal with the conflict within myself. So I remain locked in the very place from which I want to escape. I really set myself up when I don't notice what is actually good. I am so focused on what is bad so I can escape it, that I sabotage the good that I actually have. I can't seem to wrap my mind around the idea that I need to take the good with the bad. I'm too caught up in my *if only* mindset. Or, conversely, I deny the dark so I don't have to deal with it. I will be very impatient and want immediate gratification. When running is a soft defense, it is a watered down version of these traits. I think in terms of possibilities rather than limitations, but they are primarily fantastical possibilities, and I'm still absent and elusive. I need to work hard to break through the illusion of safety that the running mentality provides and stay still.

General characteristics of Mi-mi the Runner:

Soft Running: Absent, a dreamer, unavailable, unreliable, inconsistent, all over the place, out there, not in the moment, anywhere else but here, unpredictable, fickle, idealistic, flaky.

Hard Running: Abandoning, rejecting, lost, unappreciative, denying, unrealistic, ungrounded, impulsive, unstoppable, agitated, impatient, irresponsible, addicted, lost.

RECAP OF KEY CONCEPTS CHAPTERS 10, 11, AND 12

General characteristics of the protectionist responses:

Mi-mi the Fighter, the defender of Glade: (1) *soft fighting:* challenging, demanding, testy, defiant, rebellious, insolent, audacious, foolhardy, rash, disrespectful, know-it-all; (2) *hard fighting:* stubborn, unreasonable, pushy, belligerent, aggressive, unstoppable, threatening, destructive, manipulative, pugilistic, reckless.

Mi-mi the Hider, the keeper of Glade: (1) *soft hiding:* stoic, compliant, passive, predictable, safe, withdrawn, detached, distant, long suffering; (2) *hard hiding:* powerless, hopeless, incapable, complacent, resigned, defeated, pessimistic, unreadable, unknowable, deceptive, absent, victimized, fake, pretentious.

Mi-mi the Runner, the seeker of Glade: (1) *soft running:* absent, a dreamer, unavailable, unreliable, inconsistent, all over the place, out there, not in the moment, anywhere else but here, unpredictable, fickle, idealistic, flaky; (2) *hard running:* Abandoning, rejecting, lost, unappreciative, denying, unrealistic, ungrounded, impulsive, unstoppable, agitated, impatient, irresponsible, addicted.

13: TAKING CHARGE OF YOUR LIFE

The hero is he who is immovably centered.[xxii]

Your inner being guard, and keep it free.[xxiii]

You are now more aware of the protectionist mindsets of Mi-mi the Fighter, Mi-mi the Hider, and Mi-mi the Runner, so you can more easily identify them when their manners of thinking, reasoning, and emoting take over. Awareness is the first stage of reducing the boomerang effect. It begins the process of you being able to take back your own power to direct your life. You need to be able to recognize their entrapment and distortions so that you just don't follow them blindly, like a sheep following the wolf into its cave. We know where that story leads, don't we?

The next stage of taking charge of your life is to soften the protectors hold over you. To effectively do this, you need to attend to the whole self—mind, body, and emotions—to ease the sense of threat that is triggering the protectionist responses, and to create safety from within on all levels. In this chapter, you will learn exercises to help you do this. The first of these is deep abdominal breathing techniques. Emotional and mental stress overstimulates our sympathetic nervous system, resulting in increased heart rate, perspiration, and muscle tension. Our breathing is rapid and shallow. Over time, this can lead to such things as high blood pressure and muscle pain.[xxiv] The sympathetic nervous system, however, has a complementary system known as the parasympathetic nervous system, whose main purpose is to make the mind/body rest and relax. This is called the *relaxation response.*[xxv] Stimulating the parasympathetic nervous system when you perceive emotional or mental threat, so that you can diminish the protectionist response of fight, flight, or freeze, helps you to step through stress, strife, and strain. You balance out and gain a greater sense of control in the face of perceived threat.

Deep abdominal breathing is a generic technique that you can use to reduce the protectors in dominant mode. It is the first and simplest tool that you can employ to help you better manage them. The other three exercises target each individual protectionist response. They utilize mindfulness and imaging to help you soften the protectors. Mindfulness, which is the capacity to focus on our present moment without distraction, has been shown to have positive effects on our mind/body. J. David Creswell, who researches the relationship between mindfulness and stress reduction at UCLA, and his colleagues found that the more mindful we are, the more our right ventrolateral prefrontal cortex is activated, and the less the amygdala is triggered.[xxvi] The amygdala is the alarm system in our brain. In moments of threat or stress, even something as innocuous as a picture of an angry face, the amygdala activates a cascade of biological hormones to protect the mind/body. This helps explain why mindfulness programs can improve mood and health, as the prefrontal cortex may serve as a compensatory response to severe anxiety,[xxvii] and its activation reduces the activity in the amygdala. Hence, these exercises specifically target each protector and help you to balance them with mindful responses.

*

All of the exercises in this chapter are about paying attention to and taking care of yourself, mind, emotions, and body. Taking charge of your life starts with you. The exercises are five-minute self-care formulas that you can incorporate into your life to help you overcome the boomerang effect. You can do them as many times as you need or want to every day, whether once a day or at varying intervals throughout the day. You can also extend the time beyond five minutes. This formula is built on the idea that there need be no excuse or reason not to make time for the self. In a busy and demanding life, we often use limited time as the excuse for not taking care of ourselves—too busy with work, school, kids, family, watching TV, eating junk food, worrying about all of our problems....

But we must be able to find just five minutes to stop and be really good to ourselves, to focus inwards and care for our mind, emotions, and body. That way we take charge of what we can take charge of: ourselves. I invite you to open yourself to incorporating this philosophy into your daily existence. Every day, take at least five minutes to do one of the exercises in this chapter in order to take care of yourself from the inside. You can do this as many times as you want throughout your day. The goal is to integrate these exercises into your daily routine. Some days you might have several five-minute intervals. Then there will be other days when you find only one opportunity. No matter how busy, find five minutes to take care of yourself. Please know that you are very much worth the effort and time it takes to give yourself love and nurturing. Don't let anything or anyone lead you to think differently.

THE BREATH OF LIFE

Deep abdominal breathing stimulates the parasympathetic nervous system. The result is an increase in relaxation, reversing the impact of the protectionist response.[xxviii] The best part: it's free! It costs nothing and, indeed, requires little effort, just consistency and attention. Proper breathing is an essential foundation of diminishing the protectionist response. Thus, this exercise is about learning and practicing the most fundamental exercise: abdominal (also known as diaphragmic) or deep breathing. Unfortunately, most of us take shallow breaths through our chest and shoulders. We are unaware that we do this unless we learn proper deep breathing techniques through our abdomen. If you watch babies or animals breathe, for instance, you'll see that they do so with their whole bodies. Their bellies rise and fall with each inhalation/ exhalation. For reasons unknown, we stop doing this as we mature, to the detriment of our well-being. So we need to relearn how to breathe properly through our abdomen again. The good news is that this is pretty easy to do with practice.

There are many reasons why deep abdominal breathing is beneficial. Shallow breathing through our chest impedes the flow of oxygen to the brain and muscles, and delivers fewer nutrients to our tissues. When our breath is slower, fuller, and deeper, we take in more oxygen and release more carbon dioxide. Such breathing reduces the amount of stress we experience in our lives, which has positive benefits for our overall health: better circulation and blood flow, and a more efficient lymphatic system, which is an important part of immune health.

Deep breathing also helps us control feelings such as stress, anger, tension, anxiety, and pressure. We handle perceived threats better and diminish protectionism. Unless we learn to do this, however, we will chest breathe, which makes us more anxious under pressure. When we feel such things as stress, frustration, helplessness, hurt, anger, etc., we inhale shallowly through our chest and even hold our breath. This increases protectionism.

Here is a test to find out about your habit of breathing. Place one hand on your chest and the other on your stomach just below your belly button. Now inhale normally. Which rises first, your chest or your stomach? Which expands the most? If your chest rises first and expands the most, you are a chest breather. If this is true for your stomach, you are an abdominal breather.

In this upcoming exercise, you will learn abdominal breathing techniques. The exhalation is a particularly important part of this process, as it informs the mind/body that it can relax and thus subverts it away from the fight, freeze, or flight responses. Although we breathe as a part of our existence, if you are not accustomed to breathing abdominally, it will feel strange and abnormal, even uncomfortable. Do not let that deter you. Remember the good news: you can train your mind/body to breathe properly. With regular practice, you will learn to inhale and exhale through the abdomen as your normal way of breathing. As simple as breathing is, it can also be transformational with proper application. So do practice and take the time to learn it. It's easy. It just takes remembering and repetition. Use post-it notes to remind yourself to do it, for instance. Put these up at home and at work. Please remember that you are very much worth the effort and time. It is something simple that you can do to be good to yourself and take good care of you, anytime and anywhere. Time constraints don't need to hamper you. It is what you deserve. Practicing abdominal breathing techniques is a beneficial thing that you can do for your physical, mental, and emotional health, on an immediate and long-term basis.

EXERCISE 1: DEEP ABDOMINAL BREATHING

1. Place your right hand on your abdomen below your belly button and your left hand on your chest. Close your eyes.

2. Inhale slowly and deeply through your nose into your lungs, focusing your attention on where your right hand rests below your belly button. That is, imagine breathing into the place where your hand is. Your chest should not move, while your stomach expands or rises like a balloon, pushing your right hand upward. Your left hand on your chest should not rise. If it does, imagine that your left hand is keeping your chest still. You are trying to open and expand only your abdomen with your breath. Count to five as you do this.

3. Pause for a second after the full inhalation, and then exhale fully through your nose. The exhalation should be a bit longer, so count to seven or eight as you let the air out of your body. If you feel tightness around your diaphragm, do not be concerned. This just means that your muscles are taut from improper breathing. They will loosen and relax as you practice.

4. Make sure that your breathing—inhaling and exhaling—is smooth and flowing, rather than choppy. It should be one slow, long, and continual inhalation and exhalation. Do it through your nose only as a form of natural breathing.

5. Inhale and exhale at least ten times, but I encourage you to continue for up to five minutes. The longer you do it, the more relaxed you will become.

6. Practice this exercise regularly, at least once a day, for at least the next week.

Advanced Exercise 1: Lifestyle Breathing through the Abdomen

1. Lifestyle breathing through your abdomen, rather than your chest, can easily be incorporated into your daily life. You can do it anywhere and anytime (remember, it's free), such as when walking, cleaning your teeth, in the shower, driving, washing dishes, talking on the phone, at your desk, watching TV. You get the picture. This will help you when you are experiencing emotional and mental stressors as a result of the muck factor's presence. You can more easily bring your breath into focus and stimulate the relaxation response to help quiet the protectionist response.

2. You don't need to focus on the exhalation in your daily routine. Just check to make sure you are breathing into your stomach throughout the course of the day.

3. You will need to remind yourself to do this in order the train your mind/body to breathe properly. So make a point of this. For example, write yourself notes and place them on mirrors, your fridge, or other key places where you will see the reminder. Make a note to breathe in your daily calendar. Send yourself e-mail, text, or voice-mail reminders. Start the day with abdominal breathing as you go about readying yourself for it.

4. Abdominal breathing helps you to inhale life to its fullest and brings calm into your day. The reward is far greater than the small effort it takes to remember to breathe deeply through your life. Take care of your mind, emotions, body, and soul because you are worth it!

5. Abdominal breathing can be therapeutic. With practice, it can become your standard way of breathing and part of your everyday lifestyle.

6. Remember: you are worth the effort it takes to learn this simple exercise. Properly inhaling the incredible breath of life is what you so richly deserve to have. It is part of taking charge of your mind, heart, body, and soul.

EXERCISE 2: MANAGING THE FIGHTER IN YOU

Recap: The Fighter in You
Characteristics: controlling, conquering, overdoing, dominating, resistant, partial
Reasoning: "It should be."
Mantra: "It must be conquered."
The Result: struggling, rigidity, limited, stuck, stunted, angry, self-beating, frustration
Antidote: surrender, softening, letting go, giving in, being "wrong," humility.

The Fighter in you is driven by the need for control, to help manage the precarious, random, and capricious nature of the muck factor. What you are seeking through this response is to feel secure when you perceive threat or stress of any kind, be it conscious or unconscious, real or imaginary. You can counter this need by finding a healthy, positive power inside yourself, so that you feel safer and more secure from within. This buffers your sense of vulnerability and helps you deal with the core, innate conflict or vulnerability; rather than focusing on the world around you and trying to control it, so you can feel better or less threatened. You target the one thing that you do have power over: yourself. Below is an exercise to help you do that.

1. Think of a time when you felt positive, strong, and powerful, such as an academic or work achievement or a personal accomplishment. Recall that memory as vividly as possible. Feel the emotional strength inside. Write it down in the space below.

The positive incident (e.g., the day I graduated from college or the day that I won the race):

_____

_____

_____

_____

_____

_____

The emotional strength I felt as a result (e.g., confident, secure, proud, happy, successful, worthy, important, valuable, competent, etc.):

_____

_____

2. Focus on where you feel that power and strength in your mind/body (your head, throat, heart, gut, etc.). Place your hand in that area and breathe into it deeply through your abdomen, as outlined in exercise 1. Give that feeling of power a symbol that you think represents it, such as sunlight, a tree, gold, a diamond, a treasure chest, a rainbow. Write the symbol in the space below.

_____

_____

3. Take five deep breaths into your abdomen, connecting with the emotion that you experienced on that successful day. Visualize or sense the symbol of power that represents that feeling in your body. Now let that symbol melt into you. If it is something hard, allow it to soften and yield, like a liquid, so that it can be absorbed into your body. A sense of inner strength and power creates a state of intrinsic safety, which allows the Fighter in you to surrender and relax. You are able to empower the one thing that you can: yourself.

4. If you have problems visualizing the symbol, don't let that deter you. Just focus on feeling the positive emotion and expand that feeling throughout your entire mind/body. That is, imagine or sense it filling all of you up, so that your attention is on this one positive state or emotion that is creating a feeling of power, confidence, and security inside you.

5. Practice this exercise for five minutes, once or twice a day or at intervals throughout your day, as often as you need to. There is no limit to how much you can be good, loving, and positive to the self. Give yourself permission to take five minutes of self-time *every* single day. That's right—just five minutes. You can

do that. And you can add more anytime you want. Remember: It is what you so rightly deserve.

EXERCISE 3: MANAGING THE HIDER IN YOU

Recap: The Hider in You:
Characteristics: safe, withdrawn, disappearing, victimized, hidden, distant
Reasoning: "What if …?"
Mantra: "It is what it is."
The Result: masking, loss of self, helplessness, powerlessness, victimization, resignation
Antidote: openness, connecting, revealing, vulnerability, truth.

Safety is what the Hider seeks, for the muck factor's unpredictable and harsh nature can lead us to feel vulnerable and powerless. The most powerful way to create healthy safety, to counter the protectionist coping style, is by taking care of and nurturing the self through all the challenges we face. This creates security from within, rather than seeking it in the world, or hiding from the world because we believe it will harm us. If we can look after ourselves, we don't need to hide from the challenges in life, from others, or ourselves. Here is a self-care exercise to help you do that.

1. Recall a hurtful incident in your life. It can be a recent or distant memory, even going back as far as childhood. Examples might be: (a) I am five years old and I am being put down by my mother, (b) I am twenty-five and my boy/girlfriend of three years is leaving me for someone else, or (c) last week my best friend made a few critical comments that triggered my insecurity about myself. Write that incident down in the space below.

_____

_____

_____

_____

_____

_____

2. What did you feel when that incident occurred? Were you scared or hurt, angry or helpless? Did you feel sad and alone, or depressed and hopeless? Perhaps you felt ashamed, guilty, powerless, insecure, or inadequate. Allow yourself to connect with the feeling or feelings around that hurtful incident and write that in the space below.

_____

_____

_____

3. Close your eyes, take a deep breath into your belly as you learned to do in exercise 1. Recall the hurtful incident as vividly as you can, as if you were watching a movie, except you are the main character. Focus on the sense of yourself in that picture. Imagine what that hurt, sad, or insecure, etc., self-projection looks like. If you have a problem visualizing this, look at photographs of yourself and pick out one to help you imagine yourself. You can also look at yourself in the mirror, so that you have an image to draw from.

4. Now imagine stepping into that incident, as if you are time traveling, and hug the image or projection of yourself. Focus on the sensory experience, the warmth of the projected body, the softness of the skin. Massage his or her back like you would sooth another person, except you are doing this to the image of your hurt self. Specifically feel the caring emotion of the embrace, and verbally express this caring to your self-image. Be compassionate and kind, as you would be to a friend in need of nurturing. Invite him/her to hug you back. Share the love. If you have problems visualizing, you don't need to "see" your self-projection. Just sense this hurt part of yourself and that you are embracing his or her essence. Looking at a picture of yourself might make this easier to do.

5. This exercise teaches you how to take care of your emotional hurts and heal them. It helps you build a positive, loving, and

supportive relationship with your self-projection. You may find it difficult or uncomfortable to imagine embracing yourself. Conversely, your self-image may be stiff and resistant. You might find that you feel as if you are far away from yourself and can't reach your own image. If that is the case, imagine taking steps toward him/her. You might even have trouble doing this. These are signs that you do not know or are not in the habit of nurturing or taking care of yourself, but you can learn how to. Practicing this exercise will help you strengthen this new emotional muscle. Feel free to do it a few times a day. The more you do it, the more you will get accustomed to seeing yourself as being cared for. Put a picture of yourself on a wall, mirror, cupboard, computer, and when you see it, imagine hugging him or her. The picture can be a contemporary one or one from your past, even your childhood. Some people find it easier to imagine embracing their self as a child, rather than as an adult. Do whatever works for you.

6. Practice this exercise for five minutes, once or twice a day or at intervals throughout your day, as often as you need to. There is no limit to how much you can be good, loving, and positive to the self. Give yourself permission to take five minutes of self-time *every* single day. That's right—just five minutes. You can do that. And you can add more anytime you want. Remember: it is what you so rightly deserve.

EXERCISE 4: MANAGING THE RUNNER IN YOU

Recap: The Runner in You
Characteristics: escapist, moving, avoidant, dreamer, ungrounded, dissociated, out there
Reasoning: "If only ..."
Mantra: "It could be."
The Result: all over the place, avoidant, addictive, never present, anywhere but here, denial
Antidote: stillness, quiet, grounding, being in the moment, realism.

The Runner is driven by the need to escape perceived threat in order to create safety. But habitual running is only self-avoidance. We never take the time to resolve the difficult emotions and thoughts within us that cause us to feel threatened in the first place. Running means that we never take the time to be with ourselves and take care of the root causes of our problems. The way to counter this impulse is to stay still and sit with the self, *all* that the self is: the good and the bad, the happy and the sad, and the many areas in between. Facing the self is required to modify the Runner in you. You need to stay present and grounded when the Runner is taking over. The exercise below helps you to face the conflict that you are trying to escape. You let it go, and then ground yourself to create stillness from within.

1. Think of your most recent challenging experience. Recall the incident as clearly as you can. What are the feelings and emotions that surround this issue? The incident could be: (a) frustration with all the extra pressure at work, (b) gaining five more pounds, (c) not being able to get my partner to understand me, (d) boredom at home sitting there by myself with no one around. Write the incident and label those emotions in the space below.

_____

_____

_____

_____

_____

My feelings (e.g., shame, hurt, anger, resentment, inadequacy, powerlessness, fear):

_____

_____

2. Now close your eyes and breathe deeply into your belly, as outlined in exercise 1. You are moving your attention inside of yourself, following your breath. Focus on recalling this memory as vividly as possible. Who was there? What was occurring?

What was said to you? What happened in your environment? What did you feel (e.g., insecure, shamed, angry, helpless, sad)? Label that emotion and then focus intensely on that negative feeling. Where do you experience this feeling in your mind/body? Is it your chest, throat, stomach, or head, for instance? Or is it somewhere else: back or shoulders? If you have problems locating the feeling in your mind/body, assume it is in your throat, heart, or gut.

I feel the negative emotion in my:

_____

_____

3. Focus on the area of your mind/body where you experience the emotion that you perceive as negative, discomforting, or problematic. Your attention is being drawn deeper inside of you. Place your hand there. Breathe deeply into that area of your mind/body where your hand is. That is, imagine your breath going into the place in your mind/body where you feel the stressful or uncomfortable emotion. If you are unable to visualize it, just focus on breathing into that part of your mind/body where you sense the feeling exists, as if your breath is being pushed into that area. Now imagine this feeling dropping from wherever it is located into the soles of your feet. Use your breath to do this, pushing the emotion down your mind/body and into your feet. If you are good at visualizing, you can imagine a hard rock falling into your feet. If visualization is challenging for you, focus on breathing the emotion into your feet, as if you are pushing a weight that you feel but cannot see with the air of your breath.

4. Next, imagine moving the emotion out through your feet into the ground below. Use your breath to do this. If you are able to visualize it, picture this as a rock being ejected or pushed from your feet into the earth, where it disintegrates and disappears. If visualization is difficult for you, focus your attention on breathing the emotion out of your feet, sensing that it is dissipating. You

do not need to see anything. Using your senses—that is, your ability to feel as you would in a dark room, where you cannot see but can touch—let it pass out of your feet. Do this process until you feel that the emotion has completely dissolved. Keep your attention in your feet, not in your head, for grounding.

5. As the negative emotion leaves your mind/body, refocus your attention on deep breathing, feeling the air fill your mind/body and oxygenating it. Replace the emotional discomfort you just had with your breath. Keep your attention in your feet as you do this. That is, keep bringing your breath into your feet from your head, filling your whole mind/body with the breath as you do so. You are inhaling into your feet in order to ground yourself, which counters the Runner's escapist impulse. As you exhale, keep your attention in your feet as well, rather than in your head. Feel the emotional relief this brings. Focus strongly on this sense of release and grounding. Take ten of these new, fresh breaths. Open your mind/body to feel this fresh, clear, and grounded space.

6. You may notice that your attention keeps going back into your head, even if you felt the problem in your chest or belly. Please don't make that a problem, perhaps thinking that you aren't able to do the exercise or aren't doing it right. It only implies that you are too much in the habit of being in your head, and so the shift to grounding is challenging. It is the imbalance that is the problem, not the effort. You are simply returning to what you are used to doing, and you need to build this new emotional muscle. You just need to practice. So keep pushing the emotional discomfort back into your feet, letting it leave your mind/body that way. This grounds you, and takes your focus away from your head and into your base (feet), which supports you and helps to still you. This stillness and grounding allow the problem to pass through you more quickly than it would if you were mulling it over and over in your head, disconnected from your mind/body and self. Additionally, do not be concerned about getting visual impressions. They aren't necessary. The

most important thing is for you to sense and feel. If these are weak, practice will also strengthen your senses and develop these emotional muscles.

7. Practice this exercise often to build up the emotional muscle of stillness and grounding. Do it for at least five minutes, but feel free to do it for a longer period of time or as often as you like throughout the day, whenever you need to. Choose a quiet place for yourself. You can do it when lying in bed before you go to sleep at night or before jumping out of bed in the morning. Just set your alarm five minutes earlier. You can also do it during your lunch break. As you develop this emotional muscle, you can learn to utilize it anytime you need to. You can do it while you are walking, in the shower, sweeping the floor, driving.... Train yourself with small issues and build up the capacity with bigger ones. This will help you when you experience stress in your daily life. Instead of running from your discomforting emotions, you will instead ground yourself to support your emotional stressors, let go of them through your mind/body, and replace them with a greater sense of stillness, calm, and release.

TAKING CHARGE

The ubiquitous, unpredictable, and random nature of the muck factor brings with it many threats, challenges, bumps, and bruises. This means that the protectors will always be triggered in our lives, as the muck factor is woven into the very fabric of existence. So expect the protectors to go into high gear whenever you consciously or unconsciously perceive threat, be it real or imaginary. But you are now more aware of the seduction and distortions of the protectionist responses, and you will be less convinced by the tales they spin inside your mind. You also have four five-minute exercises to help you soften their hold.

Don't be surprised, however, when those testy protectors come back right after you've reined them in. They are a strong impetus and need consistent retraining. This is especially true when they have become habitual and non-discerning; that is, an unconscious part of our mentality, personality, behavior, and emotional life. Remember: to be healthy, we must continually feed ourselves a good diet. We can't eat a salad once a week, eat junk food the rest of the time, and expect that to do the trick.

The protectors are the "easy" way in short-term and specific situations, such as running from a stranger in a dark alley, fighting for your rights when the store clerk ripped you off, or hiding from your miserable neighbor because you just don't need to hear his whining again. They are quick fixes to shallow and immediate circumstances. But as long-term and generic lifestyle strategies, they become habitual and make our existence arduous.

Despite their long-term ineffectiveness, we do not see that. We easily fall under the spell of our primary instinct. The more habitual the protectors become—which comes with overuse, a trap we all fall into—it will get to the point where we feel like they are controlling us instead of us directing them. So we don't need to work to be protectionist. That mentality is ingrained and hardwired. Instead, we need to work to reduce their drives. You can start doing that through deeper awareness of their ways of being, and by making use of the exercises provided in this chapter. Yes, doing this definitely requires effort, as we so easily fall into the trap of the protectionist responses; so be aware of the protectionist ensnarement, distortion, and seduction. And do be kind to yourself when you get pulled into their trap. Don't let that stop you from continuing to work on reducing their presence and mindset.

Once again, you can do the five-minute exercises before you go to bed or first thing in the morning. Please feel free to do them more. They have no limitation. Then, keep practicing them in your daily life whenever you feel emotional or mental tension. Consistency and routine create change and help you take charge of your life. These are techniques that you can incorporate into your life to help you manage your stresses, struggles, and strains. You can do them pretty much anywhere and anytime, once you get in the habit of doing them. Breaking the circle of the boomerang effect requires a continual approach, and focusing more inside the self rather than on the world around you. There are no quick fixes, just healthy coping styles. Always remember: you are worth and deserve the effort.

Protectionist management, then, is the challenge of our existence. We need to take on this responsibility not just to free ourselves from strife and struggle, but also to be positive influences in the world, to our family and friends, to the planet so in need of care, and of course, most of all, to our often neglected selves. Be good to you, take care of you, be compassionate, kind, loving, and gracious to yourself. Yes, take charge of your life. Then turn to the world and be good to it too.

RECAP OF KEY CONCEPTS

The Nervous Systems

Parasympathetic Nervous System: The parasympathetic nervous system's purpose is to make the mind/body rest and relax.

Sympathetic Nervous System: Under conditions of stress, the sympathetic nervous system is activated, preparing the mind/body to act.

Types of Breathing

abdominal or deep breathing: Breathing from abdomen rather than chest.

chest or shallow breathing: Breathing from chest.

The Responses

the protectionist (a.k.a. stress) response: Stimulation of the sympathetic nervous system that triggers the fight, freeze, or flight responses.

the relaxation response: Stimulation of the parasympathetic nervous system that signals the mind/body to relax.

ACKNOWLEDGMENTS

My greatest gratitude goes to the countless people who have gone through the Self-Imaging Therapy™ (SIT) process with me. Without their journeys, this book could never have been written. We are always at once the teacher and the student.

I also need to thank Fern Turgeon for her artwork and support, Walter Lai for his photography, and Kelli Keiley and Nicole LeGault for their input. To my many other readers and supporters, friends and family, thanks for being there.

Thanks most of all to my precious son, Jasim, for always being a positive light every day of my life.

REFERENCES

i. Collins English Dictionary, 10th ed., s.v. "boomerang."

1: THE BOOMERANG EFFECT

ii. Florence Scovel Shin, *The Collected Wisdom of Florence Scovel Shinn: The Game of Life And How To Play It: Your Word Is Your Wand, The Secret Door To Success* (New York: Jeremy P. Tarcher/Penguin, 2009).
iii. Muck *noun* 1. moist farmyard dung, manure. 2. mire; mud. 3. filth, dirt, or slime. 4. defamatory or sullying remarks. 5. a state of chaos or confusion: *to make a muck of things*. 6. something of no value; trash. 7. Defamatory remarks. (Merriam-Webster's Collegiate Dictionary, 11th ed.)
iv. White, K.D., "Salivation: The significance of imagery in its voluntary control," *Psychophysiology* 15 (1978): 196-203.

2: MI-MI THE FIGHTER

v. Peter McWilliams, *Life 101: Everything We Wish We Had Learned About Life in School—But Didn't* (Los Angeles: Prelude Press, 1991).
vi. Walter Cannon first coined the human response to threat as "the fight or flight response" in 1929. The fight response can appear as angry, aggressive, or argumentative behavior. (H.

S. Friedman and R. C. Silver, eds., *Foundations of Health Psychology* (New York: Oxford University Press, 2007).) The fight reaction is stimulated whenever we encounter potentially dangerous situations. Adrenaline courses through the veins, and we respond with aggression or assertion.

vii. Recent research has demonstrated that anxiety regularly occurs in the absence of an identifiable stressor. (D. H. Barlow, *Anxiety and Its Disorders, Second Edition: The Nature and Treatment of Anxiety and Panic* (New York: Guilford Press, 1988).

3: THE STORY OF MERCY THE FIGHTER

viii. Mercy the Fighter is a pseudonym for a client of mine. This is an excerpt from an actual SIT session with me. The modifications are minor, for clarity and understanding.

4: MI-MI THE HIDER

ix. Henry Ward Beecher, *Plymouth Pulpit: Sermons Preached by Henry Ward Beecher* (New York: J.B. Ford and Co., 1869-78).

x. Jeffrey A. Gray proposed that the freeze response is the first in the stress response sequence. The sympathetic nervous system releases adrenaline and glucose into the blood stream at lightning speed. Freezing is qualified by terms such as hyper-vigilance, guardedness, watchfulness, and hyper-alertness. Freezing is the "stop, look, and listen" fear reaction. The survival advantage of this response is obvious. It can also appear as dissociative behavior. (B. D. Perry, R. Pollard, T. Blakely, W. Baker, and D. Vigilante, (1995) "Childhood Trauma, the Neurobiology of Adaptation and 'Use-dependent' Development of the Brain: How 'States' Become 'Traits,'" *Infant Mental Health J*, 16(4) (1995): 271-291.

5: THE STORY OF MARK THE HIDER

xi. Mark the Hider is a pseudonym for a client of mine. This is an excerpt from an actual SIT session with me. The modifications are minor, for clarity and understanding.

6: MI-MI THE RUNNER

xii. James Thurber, *Writings and Drawings* (New York: The Library of America, 1996).

xiii. The flight response is the second stress response that Walter Cannon coined in 1929. The primitive flight response can appear as addictive and withdrawing behaviors. (H. S. Friedman and R. C. Silver eds., *Foundations of Health Psychology* [New York: Oxford University Press, 2006).)

7: THE STORY OF MI-MI THE RUNNER

xiv. Mary the Runner is a pseudonym for a client of mine. This is an excerpt from an actual SIT session with me. The modifications are minor, for clarity and understanding.

8: THE THREE PROTECTORS

xv. Amy G. Arnsten, "Long-Term Stress Damages the Brain," *Washington Times*, accessed December 2, 2009, **http://www.washingtontimes.com/news/2009/dec/02/stress-damages-brain/**

xvi. The fight, freeze, and flight responses have been well documented and researched. They are activated by our bodies when a threatening situation is perceived. They trigger biochemical responses and activate the brain to instruct the body to either attack, freeze, or get out of the way, so as to avoid being a predator's target.

xvii. B. D. Perry, "Memories of Fear How the Brain Stores and Retrieves Physiologic States, Feelings, Behaviors and Thoughts from Traumatic Events," in *Splintered Reflections: Images of the Body in Trauma*, eds. J. Goodwin and R. Attias (New York: Basic Books, 1999).

xviii. R. Ader and N. Cohen, "Behaviorally Conditioned Immunosuppression," *Psychosomatic Medicine*, 37(4) (1975): 333-340.

xix. B. D. Perry, "Memories of Fear How the Brain Stores and Retrieves Physiologic States, Feelings, Behaviors and Thoughts from Traumatic Events," in *Splintered Reflections: Images of the Body in Trauma*, eds. J. Goodwin and R. Attias (New York: Basic Books, 1999).

xx. The sympathetic nervous system is more dominant than the parasympathetic nervous system.

9: THE LITTLE PEOPLE IN YOUR HEAD

xxi. Hans Selye, *The Stress of Life*, rev. ed., (New York: McGraw-Hill, 1978).

13: MANAGING THE PROTECTORS

xxii. Ralph Waldo Emerson in Richard Grossman, *The Tao of Emerson* (New York: Random House, 1997, 25).

xxiii. Lao Tse in Richard Grossman, *The Tao of Emerson* (New York: Random House, 1997, xi).

xxiv. C. Tsigos and G. P. Chrousos, "Hypothalamic-pituitary-adrenal Axis, Neuroendocrine Factors, and Stress," *Journal of Psychosomatic Research* 53 (2002): 865-871.

xxv. Herbert Bensen, a pioneer in the mind/body field at Harvard University, has provided a plethora of research about the health and emotional benefits of stimulating the relaxation response. H. Bensen, *The Relaxation Response*, (New York: HarperCollins Publishers, 2000).

xxvi. J. D. Creswell, B. M. Way, N. I. Eisenberger, and M. D. Lieberman, "Neural Correlates of Dispositional Mindfulness

During Affect Labeling," *Psychosomatic Medicine* 69 (2007): 560-565.

xxvii. C. S. Monk, E. E. Nelson, E. B. McClure, K. Mogg, B. P. Bradley, E. Leibenluft, J. R. Blair, G. Chen, D. S. Charney, M. Ernst, and D. S. Pine, "Ventrolateral Prefrontal Cortex Activation and Attentional Bias in Response to Angry Faces in Adolescents With Generalized Anxiety Disorder," *Am J Psychiatry* 163(6) (2006): 1091-1097.

xxviii. The idea of breathing has been well researched, and various studies show the health benefits of such practice. Jon Kabat-Zinn provides a practical guide to breathing and mindfulness techniques. Kabat-Zinn is founder and director of the stress reduction program at the University of Massachusetts Medical Center. He focuses on breathing and mindfulness as a means of physical and mental well-being. Jon Kabat-Zinn, *Full Catastrophe Living: Using the Wisdom of Your Body and Mind to Face Stress, Pain, and Illness,* (New York: Delacorte Press, 1990).